# Expeditions in Your Classroom
# English Language Arts

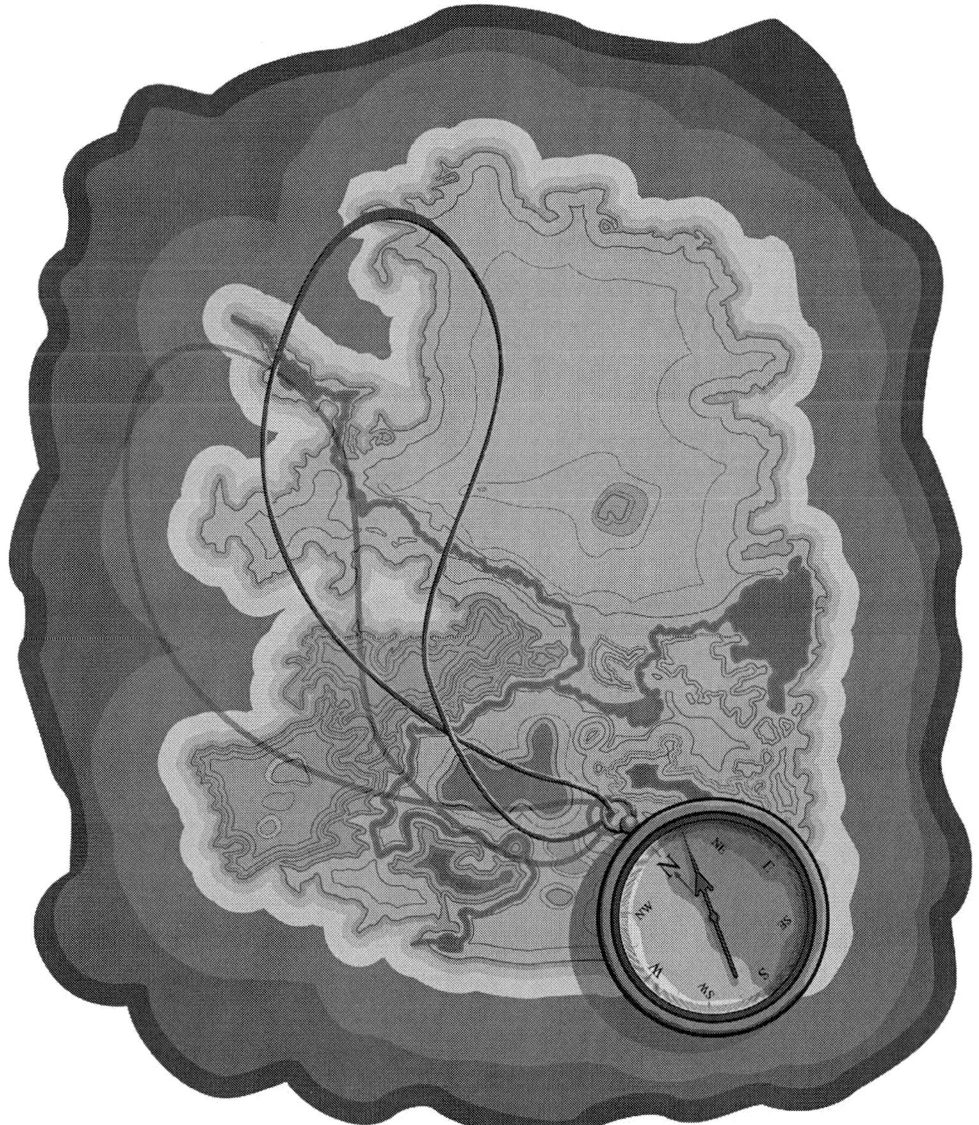

**Nora Priest**

WALCH ◣ PUBLISHING®

1     2     3     4     5     6     7     8     9     10
ISBN 978-0-8251-6270-1

Copyright © 2007

J. Weston Walch, Publisher

P. O. Box 658 • Portland, Maine 04104-0658

www.walch.com

Printed in the United States of America

# Contents

*Introduction* ............................................ *iv*

*Project Skills Chart* ............................................ *vi*

Calling All Characters ............................................ 1

The Literary Observer ............................................ 19

Community Writers ............................................ 36

Comic Literature ............................................ 52

On Air ............................................ 73

Junior Scientist Magazine ............................................ 91

Feedback, Inc. ............................................ 105

The Perfect Pitch ............................................ 124

Literary Ambassadors ............................................ 141

Point for Point ............................................ 159

English Language Arts Project Assessment Rubric ............................................ 179

# Introduction

We all remember a project we did in school, often with more vivid recall than we can summon for entire courses or years. And for good reason. Projects command attention. They force students to grapple with new information, skills, and technologies in ways that embed learning in memory. They contextualize education and help students truly understand why "I need to know that."

This book contains ten projects designed to leave a lasting mark. These projects provide students with authentic tasks involving real problems, real products, and real people, and use themes that hook young people. At the same time, they have teachers thoroughly in mind.

The high-school curriculum is packed, and, as teachers well know, a project can quickly take on a life of its own. *Expeditions in Your Classroom* provides activities and materials that scaffold student tasks, set clear criteria for final products, and offer assessment tools and a detailed outline of project steps so that teachers can focus energy on instruction rather than project management.

## About Project-Based Learning

In *Real Learning, Real Work*[1], Adria Steinberg describes the qualities of powerful projects: the six *A*'s.

**Authenticity**
Students solve problems and questions that are meaningful and real. People outside school walls tackle the same challenges. What students create and do has value beyond school.

**Academic Rigor**
Students encounter challenging material and learn critical skills, knowledge, and habits of mind essential for success in one or more disciplines.

**Applied Learning**
Students put their knowledge and skills to work in hands-on ways, and learn how to organize and manage themselves along the way.

**Active Exploration**
Students go into the field. They investigate and communicate their discoveries.

**Adult Relationships**
Students connect with adults with relevant expertise. They observe them, work with them, and get support and feedback.

**Assessment**
Students play an active role in defining their goals and assessing their progress. Adults around them give them ongoing and varied opportunities to demonstrate progress.

---

[1]Steinberg, Adria. *Real Learning, Real Work (Transforming Teaching)*. New York, NY: Routledge, 1998.

# Introduction

## Project Format and Materials

Each project contains the following materials:

### Teacher Pages

- **Overview:** information on project learning goals, prior knowledge or experience needed by students, time needed for the project, and team formation information
- **Suggested Steps:** a day-by-day view of how to deliver project activities
- **Project Management Tips and Notes:** suggestions for how to handle possible issues or information on project options and variations
- **Extension Activities:** suggested activities for extending the project or exploring related areas
- **NCTE/IRA Standards Connection:** a list of standards students will meet through the project
- **Answer Key:** answers for Before You Go and Skill Check questions

### Student Pages

- **Expedition Overview:** a description of the project challenge, learning objectives, key vocabulary terms, materials needed, and web resources students use for project activities
- **Before You Go:** lead-in activities designed to review fundamental skills or knowledge needed for the project
- **Off You Go:** activities that support the core project, including guidelines and instructions for final products or presentations
- **Expedition Tools:** handouts and worksheets associated with project activities
- **Check Yourself:** two assessment tools that students use to check skill development (practice problems or questions) and evaluate their project performance overall

An English Language Arts Project Assessment Rubric is also included and can be used with any project.

# Project Skills Chart

Projects challenge students to flex more than one mental muscle at a time and integrate skills they often see dissected and covered in discrete units of study. Each project in this book has a core skill focus, but also gives students an opportunity to practice other skills. Use this chart as a reference to help you find the best project for your needs.

C = Core skill

X = Other skills covered (sometimes optional)

| Project | Page | Grammar/mechanics | Writing skills | Creative writing | Critical reading | Communication/public speaking | Visual presentation | American literature | World literature | Literary genres/responding to literature | Research skills |
|---|---|---|---|---|---|---|---|---|---|---|---|
| Calling All Characters | 1 | | | X | C | C | X | X | | C | |
| The Literary Observer | 19 | X | C | X | C | | X | X | X | C | |
| Community Writers | 36 | C | C | | X | X | | | | | |
| Comic Literature | 52 | X | C | C | X | | | X | X | C | X |
| On Air | 73 | X | C | C | | C | | | | X | |
| Junior Scientist Magazine | 91 | X | C | | | | X | | C | | |
| Feedback, Inc. | 105 | X | | | | C | C | X | | | |
| The Perfect Pitch | 124 | X | C | X | | X | | | | | |
| Literary Ambassadors | 141 | | | | C | X | | C | C | C | X |
| Point for Point | 159 | | X | | X | C | | | | | C |

*Expeditions in Your Classroom: English Language Arts*                    ©2007 Walch Publishing

# Calling All Characters

## Overview
Students explore the art of characterization and create a 10-minute "multi-voice" monologue on a theme they choose.

## Time
Total time: 10 to 12 hours
- Before You Go—Character Study: 55 minutes in class and 60 minutes of homework
- Activity 1—Operation Observation: one to two 55-minute class periods and 60 to 90 minutes of homework
- Activity 2—Voices Monologue: three 55-minute class periods and 3 to 4 hours of homework

## Skill Focus
- characterization
- descriptive and narrative writing skills
- presentation skills

## Prior Knowledge
- analyzing prose
- story structure and elements

## Team Formation
Students work on this project individually.

## Lingo to Learn—Terms to Know
- **character:** a person or anything presented as a person in a literary work
- **characterization:** the method a writer uses to develop a character
- **direct characterization:** method in which the writer makes direct statements about a character, tells the reader what the character is like, or has another character do so
- **dynamic character development:** when a character's values, understanding, views, and so forth change during the course of the story
- **indirect characterization:** method in which the writer reveals character information through the character's thoughts, words, actions, and how others react to him or her
- **static character development:** when a character does not undergo any important internal change and is essentially the same at the beginning and end of the story

# Calling All Characters

## Suggested Steps
### Preparation

Choose three or four examples of great characterizations. Choose disparate approaches. You can use them throughout the project to inspire students. Examples include Pip's first encounter with Miss Haversham in Charles Dicken's novel *Great Expectations*, and Daniel Beaty's poem "Knock Knock" or clips from his one-man show "Emergence-SEE!" (www.danielbeaty.com/audio.html).

### Day 1

1. Give an overview of the project and review project materials.

2. Read or listen to one or two examples of good characterizations. Discuss what makes them work.

3. Review the definitions of direct versus indirect characterization and static versus dynamic character development. Ask students for examples from books and movies they know.

4. Explain Before You Go: Character Study and assign a due date.

### Homework

Have students work on Before You Go: Character Study.

### Day 2

1. Solicit examples from student character studies in progress. Discuss.

2. Consider having students pair off and help each other with their characterizations. For instance, partners can talk about how they see each other (dominant characteristics, traits, and so forth). Diplomatically provide ground rules (be kind!) or structure activities to support interaction. For example, have students come up with ten adjectives they would use to describe their partner.

3. Read aloud and discuss another example of great characterization in literature. Alternatively, discuss an example that doesn't work (choose a bad movie or television show) and why.

# Calling All Characters

**Homework**

Have students complete Before You Go: Character Study.

**Day 3**

1. Have students present their character studies.

2. Discuss each. Ask students: What is the characteristic or trait, and what evidence reveals it?

3. Explain Activity 1: Operation Observation and assign a due date.

**Homework**

Have students work on Activity 1: Operation Observation.

**Day 4—Activity 1 Due Date**

1. Ask a variety of students to read their characterizations.

2. Have students trade their characterizations with a partner and create a short role-play involving both of their characters.

3. Invite students to perform role-plays.

**Day 5**

1. Explain Activity 2: Voices Monologue (final product).

2. Assign a due date.

3. Indicate whether students should work in class, at home, or elsewhere.

**Monologue Due Date**

1. Have students perform monologues.

2. Ask students to give feedback on characters.

3. Prompt discussion by asking questions. Examples: What really helped define characters? How do they relate to the theme?

# Calling All Characters

**Final Day**

1. Have students complete the Skill Check worksheet.

2. Review answers.

3. Have students complete the Self-Assessment and Reflection worksheet and submit it (optional).

## Project Management Tips and Notes

Before students start writing their monologues, meet with each one to review plans and Monologue Prep Sheets. You may want to meet again to review the draft script.

## Suggested Assessment

Use the English Language Arts Project Assessment Rubric or the following point system:

| | |
|---|---|
| Team and class participation | 10 points |
| Expedition Tool: Character Study Notes | 10 points |
| Activity 1: Operation Observation | 20 points |
| Expedition Tool: Monologue Prep Sheet | 10 points |
| Activity 2: Voices Monologue | 45 points |
| Self-Assessment and Reflection | 5 points |

## Extension Activities

- Record or videotape monologues.
- Perform monologues in front of an audience, such as family members or another class.

## NCTE/IRA Standards Connection

3. Students apply a wide range of strategies to comprehend, interpret, evaluate, and appreciate texts. They draw on their prior experience, their interactions with other readers and writers, their knowledge of word meaning and of other texts, their word identification strategies, and their understanding of textual features (e.g., sound-letter correspondence, sentence structure, context, graphics).

4. Students adjust their use of spoken, written, and visual language (e.g., conventions, style, vocabulary) to communicate effectively with a variety of audiences and for different purposes.

# Calling All Characters

5. Students employ a wide range of strategies as they write and use different writing process elements appropriately to communicate with different audiences for a variety of purposes.

6. Students apply knowledge of language structure, language conventions (e.g., spelling and punctuation), media techniques, figurative language, and genre to create, critique, and discuss print and non-print texts.

## Answer Key
### Check Yourself! Skill Check

1. *Characterization* is creating or representing a character in an artistic work by describing or developing aspects of his or her character: appearance, background, motivations, beliefs, values, intentions, actions, and so forth.

2. An author might use physical information to convey psychological traits or a connection to a past event; use dialogue with another character; tell a story or backstory; or describe an environment or objects the character controls (home, car, and so forth).

3. An author uses events, actions, dialogue, clothing, descriptions, and so forth.

4. Answers will vary. Possible answers:
   not enough research or thought (superficial or underdeveloped characters); creating characters the reader can't relate to (they're inflexible, unbelievable, or unrealistic); bad or unnatural dialogue; too much direct characterization and using the character or another character to tell the reader what a character is like or how he is feeling (telling the reader outright "that guy is a jerk" instead of implying it indirectly by describing a moment that highlights the fact)

# Calling All Characters
## Expedition Overview

### Challenge
What are clues to your character? The things you laugh at? Your signature? How you treat a store clerk or a dog? Good authors drop clues like these and more to bind you to the heroes, villains, and other inhabitants of their fictional worlds. For this project, you will study character and characterization up close by observing yourself and people around you. You will also create characters of your own and weave their voices together into a powerful monologue you will perform.

### Objectives
- To understand how an author reveals and develops character
- To strengthen your narrative and descriptive writing skills

### Project Activities
**Before You Go**
- Character Study

**Off You Go**
- Activity 1: Operation Observation
- Activity 2: Voices Monologue

### Expedition Tools
- Character Study Notes
- Snapshot in Words
- Monologue Prep Sheet

### Other Materials Needed
- notebook
- computer with Internet access
- tape recorder (optional)

### Lingo to Learn—Terms to Know
- character
- characterization
- direct characterization
- dynamic character development
- indirect characterization
- static character development

# Calling All Characters
## Expedition Overview

### Helpful Web Resources

- Daniel Beaty
  www.danielbeaty.com

- Make 'Em Laugh!
  http://monologues.co.uk

- StoryCorps
  www.storycorps.net

- Theatre History Script Archive: Monologues
  www.theatrehistory.com/plays/monologues.html

# Calling All Characters
## Before You Go

## Character Study

> **Goal:** To understand the strategies and methods a writer uses to convey character
>
> **Tools:** Character Study Notes

### Directions

An author wants to base a character in a novel on someone special—you. She has asked to shadow you for a few days so that she can paint a realistic and detailed portrayal. She is looking for the obvious things—what you look like, how you talk—as well as illuminating behaviors and character-defining moments. She is also counting on a few surprises—things you say or do that might seem out of character or reveal character complexity.

What would she note? Remember, when it comes time to write, she will use details and clues that suggest general characteristics (indirect characterization instead of direct characterization). She doesn't want to write several pages of profile.

Imagine yourself as the author, an outside observer. "Follow" yourself for one week. Write down examples of traits, behaviors, and moments that someone might use to describe your character. Use the Character Study Notes sheet to record information. Be sure to identify the evidence that reveals the trait. Be prepared to share examples in class.

# Calling All Characters
## Expedition Tool

### Character Study Notes
Use this worksheet to help you identify key character traits and the evidence that supports them.

First impressions: _____

_____

_____

_____

Key background information/basic facts: _____

_____

_____

_____

Main personality traits: _____

_____

_____

_____

Telling actions and reactions: _____

_____

_____

_____

What others think/what he or she thinks of others: _____

_____

_____

_____

# Calling All Characters
## Off You Go

## Activity 1: Operation Observation

| | |
|---|---|
| **Goal:** | To observe people and use the details gathered to create a character sketch |
| **Materials:** | notebook, pen, computer |
| **Tools:** | Snapshot in Words worksheet |

## Directions

1. Sit in a public place such as a coffee shop, a park, a subway or bus, a movie theater, or a mall.

2. Pick out one person. Quietly and discretely observe him or her and take notes. What does the person look like? What is he or she doing? Does the person say anything? Using the eyes of a detective or a painter, write down every little detail that strikes you. Use the Snapshot in Words sheet to guide you.

3. Write a character sketch about the person. Your sketch should be three to four paragraphs long. Use your imagination to stretch the details you observed into a more complete description. Who *is* this person? For example, you might describe:

   - why the person might be at the location or what he or she might do when not there
   - what might have happened just before the person arrived or what might happen next
   - a secret dream or desire this person might have or something he or she is afraid of
   - an event that might have shaped this person's life

4. Partner with another student and describe your characters to each other. Together, imagine a scene where your two people meet. What happens? Discuss.

5. Create and write a short role-play of the encounter (3 to 4 minutes). For fun, you might imagine the people in an interesting setting or scenario, such as:

   - finding the last doughnut on a plate in the office lunchroom
   - standing on a crowded bus
   - meeting at a sporting event
   - interviewing for the same job
   - meeting on a cruise ship or travel tour
   - participating as a member of the first civilian team living in the International Space Station

# Calling All Characters
## Expedition Tool

### Snapshot in Words
Use these prompts to help you take notes during your character observation.

**Look**

How is the person dressed? What are some of his or her dominant physical features? List other interesting physical details. Does the person's appearance, style, or clothing give any clues about his or her mood or personality?

_____

_____

_____

_____

_____

**Do**

What is the person doing? Is there anything notable about _how_ he or she is moving? Is the action fast or slow? Is the activity seemingly purposeful or carefree? Are there any facial expressions or body language?

_____

_____

_____

_____

_____

**Say**

Is the person speaking? What does the person's voice sound like? Did he or she use a particular word or phrase? Describe the person's tone, pace of speech, and so forth.

_____

_____

_____

_____

_____

# Calling All Characters

## Expedition Tool

Other Observations

_____

_____

_____

_____

_____

_____

_____

_____

_____

_____

### In a Word

Write ten adjectives that capture this person (no more than five physical descriptors).

_____     _____

_____     _____

_____     _____

_____     _____

_____     _____

# Calling All Characters

## Off You Go

## Activity 2: Voices Monologue

> **Goal:** To create a 10- to 15-minute monologue that integrates the voices of three to five characters
>
> **Materials:** computer, tape recorder (optional)
>
> **Tools:** Monologue Prep Sheet

As your final assignment for the project, you will create a multi-voice monologue in which three to five characters speak separately about a theme you identify. You will script each segment and read or perform the finished piece in class.

> **Multi-Voice Monologue Guidelines**
>
> ❑ The monologue should be 10 to 15 minutes in length.
>
> ❑ Include three to five characters.
>
> ❑ Characters speak independently. No two speak at the same time (no dialogue).
>
> ❑ Retain a common theme or thread throughout the piece. Characters may speak to the theme directly or indirectly.
>
> ❑ Produce a printed/typed script for the piece.
>
> ❑ Record your final monologue, if assigned.

## Directions

1. Choose a theme or a topic. For example, you might choose an event or an emotion.

2. Brainstorm a list of people (characters) who might relate to, care about, or have a unique view or insight into your topic. These characters, however, do not necessarily have to know one another or have other obvious connections.

# Calling All Characters
## Off You Go

For example, if you choose a theme such as "memories," your list might include:

- an elderly person recalling a key event in his or her life
- a person suffering from amnesia
- someone in a crisis situation seeing life flash before his or her eyes
- a person in a psychiatrist's office

3. Use the web resources to review good monologue-writing techniques. In many ways, writing a good monologue is the same as writing a good story—only much shorter! The plot and character are all expressed through what is spoken. Some questions to ask yourself include:

- How will you hook listeners?
- How will you introduce the theme (perhaps implying it rather than saying what it is directly)?
- Is there a climax or key moment where the audience really connects with what the character has been trying to say?
- Is there an ending?

4. Use the Monologue Prep Sheet to help you outline each character and segment.

5. Write a draft of each segment. If it helps, speak it aloud into a tape recorder first, and then write.

6. Get feedback from others. Your teacher may ask you to read some of your draft material in class.

7. Prepare your final monologue. Finalize the script. If your teacher instructs, record it.

8. Present or perform your monologue in class. Your teacher may ask you to read all or part of your work.

# Calling All Characters
## Expedition Tool

### Monologue Prep Sheet

Character's name: _____

Main characteristics and traits: _____

_____

_____

_____

_____

Character's viewpoint (how character relates to my theme—perspective or relationship to it):

_____

_____

_____

_____

Main point or emotion my character should convey during the monologue:

_____

_____

_____

Segment outline (what this character will talk about): _____

_____

_____

_____

_____

Order in monologue (when this character's segment should occur): _____

_____

# Calling All Characters
## Check Yourself!

### Skill Check

1. In literary terms, what is *characterization*?

   _____

   _____

   _____

   _____

   _____

2. Describe at least five techniques an author could use to convey character in a novel or a play.

   _____

   _____

   _____

   _____

   _____

3. How does an author develop character throughout a novel or a play?

   _____

   _____

   _____

   _____

   _____

4. What problems or challenges might a writer face developing and presenting strong characters? What are common errors a writer might make?

   _____

   _____

   _____

   _____

   _____

# Calling All Characters
## Check Yourself!

## Self-Assessment and Reflection
### Project Management

### Before You Go

- ❏ I understand the concept of characterization and the different methods a writer might use to portray a character (indirect or direct, dynamic or static).
- ❏ I'm honestly not sure I can explain characterization and how a writer conveys and develops a character. I have asked my teacher for help.

### Off You Go

- ❏ I reviewed the project challenge and project materials carefully and thoroughly. I understand the requirements of products I need to create: a character study of myself, a well-written characterization of someone else, and a 10- to 15-minute monologue that integrates the voices of several characters.
- ❏ My Character Study Notes are thoughtful and legible. I provided evidence for traits.
- ❏ My character sketch is based on actual observation with my own imaginative overlay. It is descriptive and well-written.
- ❏ My Voices Monologue meets all guidelines. I got feedback on draft materials. I was well-prepared and ready to present the final version.
- ❏ I managed the Voices Monologue portion of the project effectively.

### Do You Know?

- ❏ I can define the Lingo to Learn vocabulary terms for this project and give an example of each.
- ❏ I completed the Skill Check questions and carefully reviewed questions I answered incorrectly.

# Calling All Characters
## Check Yourself!

**Reflection**

1. What were the most challenging aspects of this project for you and why?

_____

_____

_____

_____

_____

_____

_____

2. What skills did this project help you develop?

_____

_____

_____

_____

_____

_____

_____

_____

3. If you did this project again, what might you do differently and why?

_____

_____

_____

_____

_____

_____

_____

# The Literary ⊙bserver

## ⊙verview
Students analyze their own powers of literary analysis, and then create a newspaper inspired by a novel they are reading in class.

## Time
Total time: 8 to 10 hours
- Before You Go—Getting into Prose: one 55-minute class period and optional homework reading
- Activity—What's the Story?: three 55-minute class periods and 4 to 6 hours of homework

## Skill Focus
- literary analysis (elements of prose)
- critical-reading skills
- writing skills

## Prior Knowledge
Familiarity with the main elements of prose (plot, characterization, theme, and setting) is helpful.

## Team Formation
This is a class project; each student is responsible for specific contributions.

## Lingo to Learn—Terms to Know
- **characterization:** the method a writer uses to develop a character
- **plot:** the structure of a story; how events are sequenced; the action
- **setting:** the time, place, and environment in which a story unfolds
- **theme:** the underlying ideas or messages in a work

## Suggested Steps
### Preparation

- Identify the novel students will use for the project.
- Collect a few sample newspapers students can review for feature ideas.
- Decide how students will assemble the final newspaper. For instance, decide on the format (print or online), the paper size specifications, the number of student editors, and so forth.

# The Literary Observer

**Day 1**

1. Provide an overview of the project and review project materials.

2. Lead Before You Go: Getting into Prose.

3. Refresh student memory about story elements. Review definitions of plot, setting, tone, and so forth.

4. Tap into students' prior knowledge. Ask students: What does it mean to read critically? What should/could you ask yourself as you read?

5. Explore nontraditional strategies, questions, or prompts students can use to explore a particular element. Ask students: What really works for you? What is your personal analytical style?

**Day 2**

1. Explain the What's the Story? activity (final product) and review guidelines.

2. Give due dates for the proposal, draft items, and final items.

3. Distribute sample newspapers to help students brainstorm ideas.

**Homework**

Have students complete the item proposal.

**Day 3 through Draft Article Due Date**

1. Review proposals. Look for areas where students could collaborate or should revise their angle to distinguish their piece from a classmate's.

2. Check progress. Ask students to give examples of their work-in-progress.

3. Have students peer-edit to review and revise drafts.

4. Facilitate the creation of common elements such as the newspaper name, the masthead, and the staff list as a class. Have student volunteers create those elements.

# The Literary ⊙bserver

**Layout and Final Copy Days**

1. Provide instructions for assembling a draft of the paper. Students can handle layout manually by cutting and pasting or by using a computer. You might ask several students to serve as the layout team rather than working with the entire class.

   Use the following typical newspaper measurements; or, use whatever works best given your paper supplies:

   - column size: $2\frac{1}{2}$ inches, sometimes 3 inches wide

   - paper: $22\frac{3}{4}$ inches (h) × $24\frac{3}{4}$ inches (w), folded

2. Review the draft layout. Reposition articles and elements as needed. *Note:* Students may need to adjust the length of their pieces.

3. Have copy editors (students) review the final layout one last time.

4. Run the presses! Distribute the paper.

5. Ask students to read and respond to all articles and features.

**Final Day**

1. Have students complete the Skill Check questions.

2. Check and review answers.

3. Have students complete the Self-Assessment and Reflection worksheet and submit it (optional).

## Project Management Tips and Notes

- Review student article ideas. Have students collaborate on supplementary elements. For example, several students may want to do classifieds or police notes.

- You may need to assign elements or articles to students if some areas are lacking.

## Suggested Assessment

Use the English Language Arts Project Assessment Rubric or the following point system:

| | | | |
|---|---|---|---|
| Team and class participation | 20 points | Supplementary element | 25 points |
| Newspaper article | 50 points | Self-Assessment and Reflection | 5 points |

# The Literary ☉bserver

## Extension Activities

- Create a web-based e-zine instead of a newspaper.
- Visit a local newspaper.
- Invite a local editor to class to share writing and newspaper production tips.
- Use the newspaper stories as inspiration for a video-news show.

## Other Helpful Resources

- Analyzing Literature: A Guide for Students (PDF)
  http://wps.ablongman.com/wps/media/objects/327/335558/AnalyzingLit.pdf
  (You may want to review first; content is geared toward college-level students.)

## NCTE/IRA Standards Connection

2. Students read a wide range of literature from many periods in many genres to build an understanding of the many dimensions (e.g., philosophical, ethical, aesthetic) of human experience.

4. Students adjust their use of spoken, written, and visual language (e.g., conventions, style, vocabulary) to communicate effectively with a variety of audiences and for different purposes.

5. Students employ a wide range of strategies as they write and use different writing process elements appropriately to communicate with different audiences for a variety of purposes.

6. Students apply knowledge of language structure, language conventions (e.g., spelling and punctuation), media techniques, figurative language, and genre to create, critique, and discuss print and non-print texts.

# The Literary ⊙bserver

## Answer Key
### Check Yourself! Skill Check

1. Interpreting a literary work means analyzing language and themes (not just summarizing the plot and identifying characters).

2. Answers will vary. Sample answers:
   Where does the action take place? What do the places look like or sound like? What impression do they leave? How do they set the tone for the story? When does the story take place? What is the historical time period? How long does it take the story to unfold (a lifetime, a day)? What is the social context of the story? What customs, behaviors, and social mores are questioned or featured?

   Setting is the backdrop for character or action. A writer uses it to affirm, contrast, highlight, or provide clues for other elements in the story (for instance, a character).

3. Answers will vary. Possible answers:

   a.  one morning; troubled dreams; room; textile samples; dull weather

   b.  troubled dreams; horrible vermin; always rolled back to where he was

   c.  troubled dreams; horrible vermin; textile samples; traveling salesman; illustrated magazine, housed in a nice, gilded frame, etc.; sad; if I sleep longer; used to sleeping on his right; tried it a hundred times

   d.  troubled dreams/dream; shut his eyes so he wouldn't have to look at the floundering legs

# The Literary Observer

## Expedition Overview

### Challenge

There is nothing better than sending a canny investigative reporter to sniff out the real story. In this project, you will use your journalistic skills and powers of literary analysis to produce a newspaper that covers all the angles of a novel you are studying. From exposés to obituaries, you will cover all the novel news that's fit to print.

### Objectives

- To explore traditional and offbeat methods used to help analyze and respond to prose
- To strengthen your understanding of a novel the class is reading
- To practice journalistic and creative-writing skills

### Project Activities

**Before You Go**
- Getting into Prose

**Off You Go**
- Activity: What's the Story?

### Expedition Tools

- Getting into Prose Teaser Questions
- Newspaper Item Proposal

### Other Materials Needed

- computer with Internet access

### Lingo to Learn—Terms to Know

- characterization
- plot
- setting
- theme

### Helpful Web Resources

- Brock University—Critical Reading: A Guide
  www.brocku.ca/english/jlye/criticalreading.html

- The University of North Carolina at Chapel Hill: Literature
  www.unc.edu/depts/wcweb/handouts/literature.html

# The Literary ☉bserver

## Before You Go

## Getting into Prose

> **Goals:** To understand how you approach literary analysis; to learn mental techniques that help you interpret and respond to literature
>
> **Tools:** Getting into Prose Teaser Questions

## Directions

1. As a class, brainstorm tips and tricks you can use to analyze literature. Use the lines below to record what the group comes up with. Be creative! Of course, you are still looking for the traditional elements of prose writing: plot, characterization, setting, and theme.

   _____

   _____

   _____

   _____

   _____

   _____

   _____

   _____

2. What questions would help you personally get into a piece of prose? Write them on the lines below.

   _____

   _____

   _____

   _____

   _____

   _____

   _____

   _____

# The Literary Observer
## Before You Go

3. Discuss fun, practical ways you can free your imagination to analyze literary elements. Use the Getting into Prose Teaser Questions as a starting point. Think of your own questions or mental tricks and write them below.

_____

_____

_____

_____

_____

_____

_____

_____

_____

4. What is your analytical style? How do you tackle a piece of prose? What elements are you most likely to respond to (characters, plot, and so forth)?

_____

_____

_____

_____

_____

_____

_____

_____

_____

# The Literary Observer

## Expedition Tool

### Getting into Prose Teaser Questions

|  | Traditional questions | Other ways in |
|---|---|---|
| Plot | What is the main conflict or problem? Is it internal or external?<br><br>What is the climax or resolution?<br><br>How does the writer structure the plot (linear, story within a story, flashback, and so on)?<br><br>Who is telling the story? What type of voice is used (omniscient, first person, naive, unreliable) and what effect does that have?<br><br>Is the story literal or figurative? | How can I summarize this plot in a few sentences? (Boy meets girl. They fall in love. Family dynamics tear them apart.)<br><br>What is this story most like? A puzzle? A maze? Climbing a mountain so I can see the whole view? Why would the writer do that?<br><br>Is this story for real or do things stand for something else? Does everything stand for something else? |
| Characterization | What are the character's traits, motives, or values?<br><br>How are main characters revealed?<br><br>Are characters flawed?<br><br>What is the character's impact on the story?<br><br>Do characters change? How? | If this character were in a psychiatrist's office, what would he or she talk about?<br><br>How would this character's obituary read?<br><br>What would I ask this character if he or she were on the witness stand? Over for dinner?<br><br>Who is really controlling whom here? |
| Setting | What is the environment of the story (place, time, and social environment)?<br><br>Why does setting matter? What affect does it have on characters and action? | How does the setting make me feel (relaxed, depressed, and so on)?<br><br>How is the social setting like mine or not? |
| Theme | What is the central idea?<br><br>What is the thesis or argument?<br><br>What point of view do characters have on the theme? | What's the big idea, anyway?<br><br>Why did this person write this piece?<br><br>What does this piece say about the three big themes always found in literature: human nature, society, and conflict between the individual and society? |
| Writer's craft | What devices does the writer use to tell the story?<br><br>What kind of language does the writer use (sparse, complex, highly descriptive, symbolic)? | The writer wanted to write about a certain theme and leave an impression—do his or her writing techniques accomplish that?<br><br>Does this writer like certain words, phrases, or types of images? |

# The Literary Observer

## Off You Go

## Activity: What's the Story?

| | |
|---|---|
| **Goal:** | To produce a newspaper based on a novel you are reading |
| **Tools:** | Newspaper Item Proposal |
| **Materials:** | computer with Internet access |

Your class will produce a newspaper, complete with many of the features you might find in your local paper. Everything in the newspaper must be based on the novel you are reading. The possibilities are endless!

---

### Newspaper Guidelines

❑ Each student will contribute one article that is 400 to 500 words and one supplementary element. See a list of ideas on the next page.

❑ All newspaper items must be based on the novel. Articles should reference specific details, include quotes, and so forth.

❑ You should use the appropriate journalistic style and structure for the item you are writing (for instance, a hard news story, a feature article, or an opinion piece).

❑ Your final work should be typed and should include your byline (name), headlines, and any other information that would typically appear in a real newspaper.

---

## Directions

1. Brainstorm ideas for articles and supplementary elements. Use the list on the next page list to jump-start your thinking. Scan your local paper for features. Refer back to the discussion about "getting into prose" for possible story angles.

# The Literary Observer

## Off You Go

### Main Articles

- hard news story
- feature article
- human interest or personality profile
- exposé
- subject specific (business, sports, arts and entertainment, travel)
- advice column
- gossip column
- humor column
- interview
- book review written by you or by one of the characters in the book
- letter to the editor
- editorial
- obituary

### Supplementary Elements

- comics
- horoscope
- crossword or word puzzle
- classified ads
- readers' poll
- advertisement
- recipe
- community events calendar
- this day in history
- police note
- statistic of the day
- weather
- fun fact/did you know?
- photograph with caption

# The Literary Observer

## Off You Go

2. Propose your ideas using the Newspaper Item Proposal sheet.

3. Analyze the novel to collect the information you need. You may be creative, but your article should preserve the integrity of the novel's essential elements (plot, characterization, setting, themes, and so forth).

4. Create a draft of your piece. Work in coordination with other students who are writing similar columns or elements. For example, if several students are creating police notes, all should agree on a consistent format.

5. Use peer-editing strategies to review and revise drafts.

   *Tip:* Break into groups and have students in one group serve as editors while students in the other group serve as copy editors.

6. As a class, plan the layout and placement of newspaper elements. Your teacher will provide assembly instructions.

   *Tip:* You can piece out the layout manually (print, cut, and move pieces physically), or several students can serve as the layout team and work using a computer. Don't forget to give the paper a name and a masthead.

7. Assemble and read the final draft.

# The Literary Observer
## Expedition Tool

### Newspaper Item Proposal

1. Describe the article or feature you want to contribute. What topic will it cover? What angle or approach will you take? What is the format? How will your piece relate to the novel?

   _____

   _____

   _____

   _____

   _____

   _____

   _____

2. Do you have another angle in case someone else is working on this story?

   _____

   _____

   _____

   _____

   _____

   _____

   _____

3. Describe your supplementary element. What is it? How many or much will you do? (For instance, will you provide one police note or several?)

   _____

   _____

   _____

   _____

   _____

   _____

   _____

# The Literary Observer
## Check Yourself!

### Skill Check

1. What does it mean to interpret a literary work? _____

   _____

   _____

2. What types of questions might you ask to analyze the setting of a novel? Why is understanding the setting important?

   _____

   _____

   _____

   _____

   _____

   _____

   _____

   _____

   _____

   _____

3. Read the opening paragraphs of Franz Kafka's novella *The Metamorphosis*. Then answer the question that follows.

   One morning, when Gregor Samsa woke from troubled dreams, he found himself transformed in his bed into a horrible vermin. He lay on his armour-like back, and if he lifted his head a little he could see his brown belly, slightly domed and divided by arches into stiff sections. The bedding was hardly able to cover it and seemed ready to slide off any moment. His many legs, pitifully thin compared with the size of the rest of him, waved about helplessly as he looked.

   "What's happened to me?" he thought. It wasn't a dream. His room, a proper human room although a little too small, lay peacefully between its four familiar walls. A collection of textile samples lay spread out on the table—Samsa was a traveling salesman—and above it there hung a picture that he had recently cut out of an illustrated magazine and housed in a nice, gilded frame. It showed a lady fitted out with a fur hat and fur boa who sat upright, raising a heavy fur muff that covered the whole of her lower arm towards the viewer.

# The Literary ⊙bserver
## Check Yourself!

Gregor then turned to look out the window at the dull weather. Drops of rain could be heard hitting the pane, which made him feel quite sad. "How about if I sleep a little bit longer and forget all this nonsense," he thought, but that was something he was unable to do because he was used to sleeping on his right, and in his present state couldn't get into that position. However hard he threw himself onto his right, he always rolled back to where he was. He must have tried it a hundred times, shut his eyes so that he wouldn't have to look at the floundering legs, and only stopped when he began to feel a mild, dull pain there that he had never felt before.

What words or phrases provide important clues about the following elements?

a. setting: _____

_____

_____

_____

b. plot: _____

_____

_____

_____

c. characterization: _____

_____

_____

_____

d. theme: _____

_____

_____

_____

# The Literary Observer
## Check Yourself!

### Self-Assessment and Reflection
Project Management

**Before You Go**

- ❏ I understand the concept of literary analysis and can identify the main elements of prose fiction.
- ❏ I explored my own methods for reading and interpreting literature and have identified ways I can improve my analytical skills.
- ❏ I'm honestly not sure I understand how to analyze prose and have asked my teacher for additional help.

**Off You Go**

- ❏ I reviewed the project challenge and project materials carefully and thoroughly. I understand the products I will produce: a newspaper article and a supplementary element based on a novel.
- ❏ I participated actively in our class discussion on analyzing prose. I shared examples of methods and questions I use to understand a piece of literature.
- ❏ I reviewed newspapers for models of articles and elements I could contribute to our newspaper project.
- ❏ I developed a unique angle or approach with my items.
- ❏ I worked collaboratively with other students writing similar supplementary elements. We agreed on a common format.
- ❏ My items definitely elaborated on a specific aspect of the novel.
- ❏ I checked my written work and corrected any errors in grammar, spelling, or punctuation.

**Do You Know?**

- ❏ I can define the Lingo to Learn vocabulary terms for this project and give an example of each.
- ❏ I completed the Skill Check questions and carefully reviewed questions I answered incorrectly.

# The Literary Observer
## Check Yourself!

### Reflection

1. What were the most challenging aspects of this project for you and why?

   _____

   _____

   _____

   _____

   _____

   _____

   _____

2. What skills did this project help you develop?

   _____

   _____

   _____

   _____

   _____

   _____

   _____

3. If you did this project again, what might you do differently and why?

   _____

   _____

   _____

   _____

   _____

   _____

   _____

# Community Writers

## Overview
Students propose a community writing project that allows them to create written material someone in their community could use.

## Time
Total time: 8 to 14 hours

- Before You Go—Grammar Gaffes and Sentences with Style: one to two 55-minute classes

- Activity—Taking It to the Streets: three 55-minute classes and 5 to 8 hours of homework

## Skill Focus
- reviewing grammar and sentence structure
- analyzing writing for different audiences
- writing for a purpose
- editing and revising writing

## Prior Knowledge
- writing for a variety of audiences
- basic grammar and mechanics
- types of sentences
- peer editing

## Team Formation
Students may work individually or in pairs.

## Lingo to Learn—Terms to Know
- **active voice:** verb form in which subject performs the action
- **comma splice/run-on sentence:** compound sentence that is not punctuated correctly; two or more complete sentences (independent clauses) joined incorrectly by a comma
- **complex sentence:** a sentence with one independent clause and at least one dependent clause
- **compound sentence:** two or more independent clauses joined by a conjunction
- **dangling or misplaced modifier:** a descriptive word, phrase, or clause that is positioned incorrectly so that it appears to modify the wrong word or phrase
- **faulty parallelism:** when two or more parts of a sentence don't use similar linking words and grammatical structure (parallel structure)
- **passive voice:** verb form in which subject receives the action
- **simple sentence:** a single clause

# Community Writers

## Suggested Steps

### Preparation

- Collect samples of written material from around the community.
  Examples: a brochure from a doctor's office or a business, a business letter, a theater program, an activities guide
- Write common grammatical errors on strips of paper (see Helpful Web Resources for a link to the ten most common grammatical errors). Identify common grammatical errors made by your students in particular and include them. Put the strips in a cup, a hat, or a bowl for students to choose from.
- Get a copy of Karen Elizabeth Gordon's *The Deluxe Transitive Vampire: A Handbook of Grammar for the Innocent, the Eager and the Doomed* or *The New Well-Tempered Sentence: A Punctuation Handbook for the Innocent, the Eager and the Doomed.* Use examples to inspire students for the first activity.

### Day 1

1. Give an overview of the project and review project materials.

2. Begin Before You Go: Grammar Gaffes and Sentences with Style. Have students choose a common error from a cup, a hat, or a bowl. For fun, vote on the best or most memorable sentences.

3. If additional class time is available, continue the Before You Go activities. Distribute sample written materials, one item per group. If time is limited, assign this activity for homework and ask students to find their own writing samples. Discuss why people use different writing styles. For example, business communication often uses short sentences and bulleted points. Science writing often uses the passive voice.

### Homework

Have students work on writing sample analysis if needed.

### Day 2

1. Explain the Taking It to the Streets activity (final product).

2. Provide due dates for the proposal, draft, and final piece. Indicate whether students will work in class, at home, or elsewhere.

# Community Writers

**Proposal Due Date**

1. Ask students to describe their ideas in small groups or to the class.

2. Discuss as needed.

3. Collect and review proposals.

**Draft Due Date**

1. Have each student exchange his or her project "copy" with another student for review. Repeat if feedback from multiple students is helpful.

2. Encourage students to give substantive comments and proofreading support. Model strategies for constructive criticism and comments students might make. For example, "I like the way you described that element. What other words could you use?"

**Final Product Due Date**

1. Showcase products around the class. Use an "art gallery" format—students browse, then comment.

2. Allow time for each student to present his or her piece. Ask students to tell who in the community would use the materials and how.

**Final Day**

1. Have students complete the Check Yourself! Skill Check worksheet.

2. Review answers.

3. Have students complete the Check Yourself! Self-Assessment and Reflection worksheet and submit it (optional).

## Project Management Tips and Notes

Meet with each student about his or her community writing project proposal. Students come up with interesting ideas. Be sure projects are authentic (they involve something community members need or use) and include a meaningful writing activity.

# Community Writers

## Suggested Assessment

Use the English Language Arts Project Assessment Rubric or the following point system:

| | |
|---|---|
| Team and class participation | 10 points |
| Before You Go: Grammar Gaffes and Sentences with Style | 10 points |
| Community Writing Project Proposal | 25 points |
| Writing project copy | 20 points |
| Final product | 30 points |
| Self-Assessment and Reflection | 5 points |

## Extension Activities

- Encourage students to keep their eyes open for examples of grammar gaffes while reviewing community materials. Put examples on the classroom wall.
- Ask students to identify a community member who will evaluate student work. Prepare a simple evaluation form (overall impression, appropriateness of writing style, grammar, spelling, punctuation, and so forth).

## NCTE/IRA Standards Connection

1. Students read a wide range of print and non-print texts to build an understanding of texts, of themselves, and of the cultures of the United States and the world; to acquire new information; to respond to the needs and demands of society and the workplace; and for personal fulfillment. Among these texts are fiction and nonfiction, classic and contemporary works.

4. Students adjust their use of spoken, written, and visual language (e.g., conventions, style, vocabulary) to communicate effectively with a variety of audiences and for different purposes.

5. Students employ a wide range of strategies as they write and use different writing process elements appropriately to communicate with different audiences for a variety of purposes.

8. Students use a variety of technological and information resources (e.g., libraries, databases, computer networks, video) to gather and synthesize information and to create and communicate knowledge.

11. Students participate as knowledgeable, reflective, creative, and critical members of a variety of literacy communities.

# Community Writers

## Answer Key
### Check Yourself! Skill Check

1.  a.  error: misplaced modifier

    revision: Sitting for the first time that day, he felt immense relief.

    b.  error: comma splice

    revision: One way to crack a nut is to use a nutcracker; another way is to drop a rock on it.

    c.  error: faulty parallelism, incorrect verb tense shift

    revision: The dog spent the day lounging in the yard, watching the squirrels chatter, and jumped into action as soon as the postman arrived.

    d.  error: unnecessary use of passive voice

    revision: The priceless diamond had been stolen and the police could do nothing about it.

2.  Original paragraph:

    I had been familiar with that street for years, and had always supposed it was a dead level; but it was not, as the bicycle now informed me, to my surprise. The bicycle, in the hands of a novice, is as alert and acute as a spirit-level in the detecting of delicate and vanishing shades of difference in these matters. It notices a rise where your untrained eye would not observe that one existed; it notices any decline which water will run down. I was toiling up a slight rise, but was not aware of it. It made me tug and pant and perspire; and still, labor as I might, the machine came almost to a standstill every little while. At such times the boy would say: "That's it! Take a rest—there ain't no hurry. They can't hold the funeral without you."

*Expeditions in Your Classroom: English Language Arts*

# Community Writers
## Expedition Overview

### Challenge
You live in a community of writers. People around you use words every day to do business, raise awareness, provide vital information, entertain, honor, provoke, and more. For this project, you will identify a way to take your words out into the community. You will create written material—you decide what—that can be used by you or by someone else, where words and how you write them will really count.

### Objectives
- To learn to avoid common grammar mistakes
- To analyze writing styles used in a variety of everyday materials
- To create authentic material that could be used in your community

### Project Activities
**Before You Go**
- Grammar Gaffes and Sentences with Style

**Off You Go**
- Activity: Taking It to the Streets

### Expedition Tools
Community Writing Project Proposal

### Other Materials Needed
- computer
- Other materials will vary by project and may include a digital camera, art supplies, and so forth. Students will specify this information in their proposals.

### Lingo to Learn—Terms to Know
- active voice
- comma splice/run-on sentence
- complex sentence
- compound sentence
- dangling or misplaced modifier
- faulty parallelism
- passive voice
- simple sentence

# Community Writers
## Expedition Overview

### Helpful Web Resources
- Houghton Mifflin: 8 Common ESL Errors—and How to Correct Them
  http://college.hmco.com/devenglish/fawcett/evergreen/7e/students/esl_errors.html

- Houghton Mifflin: 10 Most Common Grammar Errors—and How to Avoid Them
  http://college.hmco.com/devenglish/fawcett/evergreen/7e/students/grammar_errors.html

- The OWL at Purdue: Sentence Variety
  http://owl.english.purdue.edu/owl/resource/573/01

- University of Colorado at Boulder: Style Guide—Proofreader's and Editor's Symbols
  www.colorado.edu/Publications/styleguide/symbols.html

# Community Writers

## Before You Go

## Grammar Gaffes and Sentences with Style

| | |
|---|---|
| **Goal:** | To understand common grammatical errors and how to avoid them; to analyze the structure and style of sentences used in a variety of written materials |
| **Materials:** | examples of written material from around the home and the community |

## Directions

1. Choose a common grammatical error from the cup or the hat provided by your teacher.

2. Work with one or two other students and review the error. Use the chart below to write an original sentence that illustrates the error. Rewrite the sentence correctly.

3. Swap with the group next to you and repeat the process. Use your best verbal artistry to concoct sentences that are impossible to forget!

| Error | Grammar gaffe | Good grammar |
|---|---|---|
| | | |
| | | |
| | | |
| | | |
| | | |
| | | |
| | | |
| | | |
| | | |
| | | |

# Community Writers

## Before You Go

4. Your teacher will give your group a piece of written material—something that you would find at home or in the community. Your job is to analyze its style. Is the piece succinct like a police report? Is it indirect and passive? Is it overflowing with adjectives? Choose one to two representative paragraphs and put sentences under close inspection. Use the chart below to help you analyze them.

| Sentence | Number of words in sentence | Type of sentence (simple, compound, etc.) | Verb style (linking, passive, active) | Descriptive words (adjectives, adverbs) |
|---|---|---|---|---|
| 1 | | | | |
| 2 | | | | |
| 3 | | | | |
| 4 | | | | |
| 5 | | | | |
| 6 | | | | |
| 7 | | | | |
| 8 | | | | |

5. What is the overall structure of the piece (inverted pyramid, straight narrative, persuasive, and so forth)? How is the information organized?

_____

_____

_____

_____

_____

# Community Writers

## Before You Go

6. How would you characterize the style of the piece? Does it fit the purpose, message, and intended audience? How?

_____

_____

_____

_____

_____

_____

7. How would you rate the piece overall? Is there anything you would revise? Why or why not?

_____

_____

_____

_____

_____

_____

# Community Writers

## Off You Go

## Activity: Taking It to the Streets

| | |
|---|---|
| **Goal:** | To create a polished piece of written material that can be used in your community |
| **Tools:** | Community Writing Project Proposal |
| **Materials:** | computer; other materials will vary by project |

Your mission is simple: Find something in the community that needs writing or rewriting, and do it!

---

**Community Writing Project Guidelines**

❑ Your project must involve an acceptable quantity of writing (not a few words on a giant poster).

❑ Your teacher must approve your proposal.

❑ Your material should be authentic so that someone in the community can, or will, actually use it.

❑ You will create a presentation of your material and present it to the class.

---

## Directions

1. Brainstorm ideas. Search the community for interesting materials and opportunities. You might consider the following:

   - advertising materials
   - a public service brochure (for example, health and safety tips, activities for young children, issue advocacy, and so forth)
   - explanatory notes for pieces in a photography, art, or museum exhibit
   - a newspaper editorial
   - description cards for products (for instance, in a jewelry, crafts, or food store)
   - liner notes for a local musician's CD
   - a brochure about a local historical site or person

# Community Writers

## Off You Go

2. Propose your idea. Use the Community Writing Project Proposal sheet to outline what you want to do.

3. Conduct research as necessary and compose your first draft. Only the text is necessary at this stage. If your project involves layout and design work (sidebars, images, and so forth), simply label the text so that it is clear what it is and where it belongs. Add notes in brackets to indicate image placement.

4. Put your draft through the editorial process. Swap a copy with another student and review each other's work. Proofread for mistakes in grammar, punctuation, and spelling. Assess whether or not the piece achieves its objective effectively (assess the style, clarity, message, audience appropriateness, and so forth). What works best? What could be refined?

5. If possible, get feedback on your piece from a community person who might actually use it.

6. Make revisions. Create your final product and present it to the class.

# Community Writers

## Expedition Tool

### Community Writing Project Proposal

1. What is your idea? What writing is involved?

   _____
   _____
   _____
   _____
   _____

2. Describe the final product clearly.

   _____
   _____
   _____
   _____
   _____

3. What steps will you take to complete the project? (For instance, will you conduct interviews, perform research, compose multiple drafts?)

   _____    _____
   _____    _____
   _____    _____
   _____    _____
   _____    _____

4. What materials and/or support do you need? Be specific.

   _____    _____
   _____    _____
   _____    _____
   _____    _____

# Community Writers
## Check Yourself!

### Skill Check

1. Practice your editing skills. What is wrong with each of the following sentences? Identify the problem and then revise the sentence.

   a. Sitting for the first time that day, his relief was immense.

   error: _____

   revision: _____

   _____

   b. One way to crack a nut is to use a nutcracker, another way is to drop a rock on it.

   error: _____

   revision: _____

   _____

   c. The dog spent the day lounging in the yard and watched the squirrels chatter, and jumped into action as soon as the postman arrived.

   error: _____

   revision: _____

   _____

   d. The priceless diamond had been stolen and there was nothing the police could do about it.

   error: _____

   revision: _____

   _____

2. This excerpt from Mark Twain's essay "Taming the Bicycle" has had most of the punctuation removed. Edit it so that it is grammatically correct. There is no single correct version; there are several ways you might handle a particular grammatical issue.

   I had been familiar with that street for years and have always supposed it is dead level but it was not as the bicycle now informed me to me surprise. The bicycle in the hands of a novice is as alert and acute as a spirit-level in the detecting of delicate and vanishing shades of difference in these matters. It notices a rise where your untrained eye would not observe that one exists it notices any decline which water will run down. I was toiling up a slight rise but was not aware of it. It made me tug and pant and perspire and still labor as I might the machine came almost to a standstill every little while. At such times the boy would say that's it take a rest there ain't no hurry. They can't hold the funeral without you.

# Community Writers

## Check Yourself!

### Self-Assessment and Reflection
**Project Management**

**Before You Go**

- ❑ I can identify common grammar errors and correct them.
- ❑ I understand how to analyze sentence structure and style.
- ❑ I'm honestly not sure I understand grammar and sentence structure fundamentals and have asked my teacher for additional help.

**Off You Go**

- ❑ I reviewed the project challenge and project materials carefully and thoroughly. I understand the requirements of my Community Writing Project and proposal.
- ❑ I gave my writing project some thought. I scanned my community for interesting materials and opportunities.
- ❑ My proposal is thorough. I defined the final product clearly and outlined all of the major steps I will take.
- ❑ My draft copy was complete and ready by the deadline.
- ❑ I carefully reviewed my partner's copy and provided substantive feedback as well as proofreading support.
- ❑ My final product is of the highest quality. It could be handed out in my community today! There are no mistakes in grammar, punctuation, or spelling.

**Do You Know?**

- ❑ I can define the Lingo to Learn vocabulary terms for this project and give an example of each.
- ❑ I completed the Skill Check questions and carefully reviewed questions I answered incorrectly.

# Community Writers

## Check Yourself!

### Reflection

1. What were the most challenging aspects of this project for you and why?

_____

_____

_____

_____

_____

_____

_____

2. What skills did this project help you develop?

_____

_____

_____

_____

_____

_____

_____

3. If you did this project again, what might you do differently and why?

_____

_____

_____

_____

_____

_____

_____

# Comic Literature

## Overview

Students learn about literary humor by exploring its history and forms. They evaluate examples of humor in film or television. They create a comic scene based on literature they are reading.

## Time

Total time: 12 to 15 hours

- Before You Go—Oh, the Humor: two 55-minute classes and 45 minutes of homework

- Activity 1—Lighten Up the Screen: 30 to 60 minutes of homework and one 55-minute class

- Activity 2—Spoofs and Goofs: three to four 55-minute classes and 4 to 6 hours of homework

## Skill Focus

- literary humor
- critical reading
- research
- creative-writing skills
- oral-presentation skills

## Prior Knowledge

Some exposure to Greek comedy and tragedy (concepts or actual works) will be helpful.

## Team Formation

Initial activities are done as a class, in small groups, or independently. Comic scene is done in teams of two to four students (can vary by team).

## Lingo to Learn—Terms to Know

- **caricature:** ludicrous exaggeration of the peculiarities or defects of a person or thing
- **comedy:** a literary work that amuses and ends happily (or ends well)
- **farce:** a play based on a humorous situation (versus character development)
- **humor:** a quality that causes amusement
- **hyperbole:** exaggeration or overstatement; hype
- **irony:** the reverse of what is expected; the contrast between what is said and what is meant

# Comic Literature

- **parody:** a literary work that imitates the style of another literary work
- **play on words (wordplay):** turn of phrase with a double meaning, a pun; a humorous use of language
- **rule of three:** technique in humor writing or joke-telling in which you use a pattern of three to structure comedic delivery (e.g., two straight lines/elements to set up the action or joke, followed by the funny element, punch line, or unexpected twist)
- **satire:** literature designed to ridicule the subject of the work; not intended to amuse
- **wit:** intellectual humor or keenness; the ability to express things in an ingeniously humorous way

## Suggested Steps
### Preparation

- Choose two or three literary passages or poems that use humor as examples for students. Alternatively, select short pieces the class can read together to kick off the project. For instance, choose a literary piece (an essay, a short story) and a humor column (by Dave Barry, Art Buchwald, and so forth). See Possible Literature Connections.
- Write forms of humor on strips of paper. Place them in a cup, a hat, or an envelope for students to choose from. See Before You Go: Oh, the Humor.
- Review Before You Go: Oh, the Humor. Be prepared to lead a discussion on the questions.
- Consider how students will form groups.

### Day 1

1. Give an overview of the project and review project materials.

2. Begin Before You Go: Oh, the Humor. Ask students if they can name different types of humor.

3. Form groups of two or three students. Allow each group to choose a type of humor from a cup, a hat, or an envelope. Have students try to define their words.

4. Review definitions as a class.

5. Ask each group to demonstrate their form of humor. Give each group a role-play scenario or let them choose.

6. Begin to discuss questions on Expedition Tool: Literary Humor.

7. Assign more in-depth humor research for homework.

# Comic Literature

**Homework**

Have students research humor types and search for an example.

**Day 2**

1. Discuss research findings and examples. Continue discussion of Literary Humor questions.

2. Share your own examples.

3. Have students swap examples and read them.

4. Assign Activity 1: Lighten Up the Screen for homework. Alternatively, you might show and discuss scenes from film or television together as a class.

**Day 3**

1. Discuss film or television examples.

2. Explain Activity 2: Spoofs and Goofs (final product). Review comedic scene guidelines.

3. Divide students into teams or allow students to create their own.

4. Give due dates for the draft, final script, and performance. Indicate whether students will work in class, at home, or elsewhere.

**Day 4 through Performance Day**

1. Give students an opportunity to "workshop" their drafts in class. They can do this within their teams, or one team could support another.

2. Outline any performance requirements (specify if props are okay, if there is a time limit, if students should memorize lines or work with scripts, and so forth).

3. Watch performances.

4. Ask students to provide feedback using the Comedic Scene Feedback form. Discuss results.

5. Allow students to revise final scripts if desired and collect.

# Comic Literature

**Final Day**

1. Have students complete the Skill Check questions.

2. Check and review answers.

3. Have students complete the Check Yourself! Self-Assessment and Reflection worksheet and submit it (optional).

## Project Management Tips and Notes

You could spread this project out over a semester or a year; for instance, have each group sign up to do a comedic scene for one of the novels the class will study. Space presentations out accordingly. This might provide some welcome comic relief from typically heavy high-school literature reading.

## Possible Literature Connections

Aristophanes: *The Frogs* or *Clouds*

Aristotle: *Poetics* (Part V on humor)

Isaac Asimov: *Isaac Asimov's Treasury of Humor* or *Asimov Laughs Again*

W. H. Auden: "For the Time Being" (poem)

Jane Austen: *Pride and Prejudice* (Mr. Collins proposing to Elizabeth)

Stephen Vincent Benét: *The Devil and Daniel Webster*

Lewis Carroll: *The Hunting of the Snark* or any work

Miguel de Cervantes: *Don Quixote*

commedia dell'arte

Joseph Heller: *Catch-22*

O. Henry: "Confessions of a Humorist" (short essay)

Marietta Holley: "Samantha" books

Langston Hughes: *The Best of Simple*

Menander (Greek New Comedy): *Dyskolos* (*The Grouch*)

Moliere: *The School for Wives*

Ogden Nash: any poem

# Comic Literature

George Orwell: *Animal Farm*

Plautus: *Miles Gloriosus* (*The Boastful Soldier*)

Shakespeare: *The Comedy of Errors* (his first comedy)

John Steinbeck: *Cannery Row* (the great frog hunt)

Jonathan Swift: *Gulliver's Travels, A Modest Proposal, The Battle of the Books*

James Thurber: "The Night the Bed Fell," "The Dog Who Bit People" (short stories)

Mark Twain: any work (try *The Diaries of Adam and Eve*)

Royall Tyler: *The Contrast* (first comedy in United States produced by professional theater company)

Evelyn Waugh: *The Loved One*

Oscar Wilde: *The Importance of Being Earnest*

P. G. Wodehouse: *Right Ho, Jeeves* (*Jeeves* series) or *Plum Pie* (short stories)

## Suggested Assessment

Use the English Language Arts Project Assessment Rubric or the following point system:

| | |
|---|---|
| Team and class participation | 15 points |
| Humor research | 15 points |
| Activity 1: Lighten Up the Screen | 15 points |
| Activity 2: Spoofs and Goofs | 50 points |
| Self-Assessment and Reflection | 5 points |

## Extension Activities

- Perform sketches for another class or audience, or make a video of them.
- Research the psychological aspects of humor and laughter (Freud).
- Explore the influences of classical comedies on later works. (for instance, the influence of Plautus' work on Shakespeare's *Comedy of Errors*, Moliere's *The Miser*, and Sondheim's musical *A Funny Thing Happened on the Way to the Forum*)

# Comic Literature

## NCTE/IRA Standards Connection

1.  Students read a wide range of print and non-print texts to build an understanding of texts, of themselves, and of the cultures of the United States and the world; to acquire new information; to respond to the needs and demands of society and the workplace; and for personal fulfillment. Among these texts are fiction and nonfiction, classic and contemporary works.

2.  Students read a wide range of literature from many periods in many genres to build an understanding of the many dimensions (e.g., philosophical, ethical, aesthetic) of human experience.

5.  Students employ a wide range of strategies as they write and use different writing process elements appropriately to communicate with different audiences for a variety of purposes.

6.  Students apply knowledge of language structure, language conventions (e.g., spelling and punctuation), media techniques, figurative language, and genre to create, critique, and discuss print and non-print texts.

## Answer Key
**Expedition Tool: Literary Humor**

1.  Answers will vary.

2.  Common forms of humor include satire, parody, farce, hyperbole, irony, and caricature. Other answers will vary.

3.  Answers will vary. Sample answers:
    the buffoon, the imposter, the trickster, the self-deprecator, the fool, the clown, the "straight man"

4.  Yes, humor is subjective and contextual. It depends on the perspective of the audience/listeners and often relates to social norms, familiar situations, geography, culture, and so forth. It can also vary by age; for example, jokes and slapstick might appeal to younger children, while satire might appeal to a more sophisticated audience.

5.  from the Greek *humours* ("juice" or "sap"), a medical term, believed to be the mix of fluids that control human health and emotion

# Comic Literature

6. Comedy involves a comic hero who appears somewhat ridiculous and reforms, is reformed, or becomes more self-aware (individual adjusts to the ideal). Tragedy involves the downfall of a great person, caused by a character flaw or conflict with some higher power. Both involve a reversal of fortune or situation.

7. Answers will vary.

8. Answers will vary.


**Check Yourself! Skill Check**

1. relevance, surprise/twist, presentation

2. Satire is witty and clever criticism of a person, an event, or an idea or the use of irony, sarcasm, or ridicule to expose, denounce, or deride vice or folly.

   Examples:
   - Jonathan Swift's *Gulliver's Travels* satirizes British society, European government, and human pettiness (also a parody).

   - Cervantes' *Don Quixote* gives a satirical view of chivalry and courtly love (also a parody).

   - Mark Twain's *Huckleberry Finn* satirizes the moral values of the antebellum South

   - George Orwell's *Animal Farm* satirizes totalitarianism.

   Parody is humorous or satirical imitation of a serious piece of work (or elements or characters in it) in order to spoof it, poke fun at it, or ironically comment on it.

   Examples:
   - John Dryden's poem "MacFlecknoe" is based on Virgil's *Aeneid*.

   - Lewis Carroll's *Alice in Wonderland* parodies Victorian schooling.

   - James Joyce's *Ulysses* is based on Homer's *The Odyssey*.

   Parody and satire are often used together.

3. Answers will vary.

# Comic Literature
## Expedition Overview

### Challenge

Can you picture Aristotle laughing so hard that he spits out his *kykeon* (barley water)? While we don't know if that really happened, we do know that Aristotle gave humor plenty of thought. He called humor "educated insolence"—meaning that humor is a bit subversive and inextricably linked to knowledge. To poke fun at the world, you have to know it. During this project, you will explore the roots of humor in history and literature and then put your own comedic powers to the test.

### Objectives

- To explore types of literary humor and the history of humor in literature
- To analyze the use of humor in writing, television, and film
- To write and perform a scene that uses elements of literary humor

### Project Activities

**Before You Go**
- Oh, the Humor

**Off You Go**
- Activity 1: Lighten Up the Screen
- Activity 2: Spoofs and Goofs

### Expedition Tools

- Literary Humor
- Comedic Scene Feedback form

### Other Materials Needed

- computer with Internet access
- television/DVD player (optional)
- Other materials will vary by project (for example, props for comedic scenes).

### Lingo to Learn—Terms to Know

- caricature
- comedy
- farce
- humor
- hyperbole
- irony
- parody
- play on words/wordplay
- rule of three
- satire
- wit

# Comic Literature
## Expedition Overview

## Helpful Web Resources

- About.com: Humor—Funny or Laughable Literature
  http://classiclit.about.com/od/humo1/Humor_Funny_or_Laughable_Literature.htm

- American Comedy Institute: The Art and Craft of Comedy
  www.comedyinstitute.com/comedyblog.html

- Dictionary of the History of Ideas: Sense of the Comic
  http://etext.virginia.edu/cgi-local/DHI/ot2www-dhi?specfile=/texts/english/dhi/dhi.o2
  w&act=text&offset=3476469&query=humor&tag=SENSE+OF+THE+COMIC

- Emerson College: American Comedy Archives
  www.emerson.edu/comedy

- The University of North Carolina at Chapel Hill: Library of Southern Literature—Humor
  in Literature
  http://docsouth.unc.edu/southlit/humor.html

- MSN Encarta: The Funniest Jokes in History
  http://encarta.msn.com/column_humormain_tamimhome/The_Funniest_Jokes_
  in_History.html

- The Paris Review: Interviews
  www.theparisreview.org/literature.php

# Comic Literature

## Before You Go

## Oh, the Humor

| | |
|---|---|
| Goal: | To learn about the history of humor in literature and the types of literary humor |
| Materials: | computer with Internet access |
| Tools: | Literary Humor worksheet |

## Directions

1. Choose one of the following types of humor from the container provided by your teacher: satire, parody, farce, hyperbole, irony, or caricature.

2. Try to define the term you chose. Have you heard it before? Review definitions as a class.

3. Use one of the following scenarios to demonstrate your form of humor. Take a few minutes to sketch out your scene and then perform it for the class.

   - a conversation between a parent and a child
   - a case of mistaken identity
   - an encounter with a landlord
   - meeting an international visitor or traveling to a foreign country for the first time
   - a patient visiting the doctor
   - an advertisement for a product

4. Use your Expedition Tool: Literary Humor to guide you in researching your type of humor. Find out more about its etymology and history, as well as about writers of this form and humor in general.

5. Find an example of your form of humor in literature. Consider which writers are masterful at writing using this form. Select a passage that shows the form in action. Read it carefully and bring a copy to class. Be prepared to explain why it is a great example.

# Comic Literature
## Expedition Tool

### Literary Humor

Use your classroom discussions, web resources, and reading to answer the questions below.

1. What makes something funny? What do funny books and movies have in common? Why can something be funny to you and not to someone else?

   _____

   _____

   _____

   _____

   _____

2. What are common forms of humor? Are there forms of humor that were used in the past that are less popular today? What are some outdated forms of humor? Why do you think they are less popular today?

   _____

   _____

   _____

   _____

   _____

3. What are some archetypal comic characters?

   _____

   _____

   _____

4. Has the idea of comedy changed through the ages? Why does comedy vary from culture to culture?

   _____

   _____

   _____

   _____

   _____

# Comic Literature
## Expedition Tool

5. What are the origins of the word *humor*? _____

_____

_____

6. How do the classic notions of "comedy" and "tragedy" in literature compare?

_____

_____

_____

_____

7. What form of humor did you research? What is the definition? How did its name originate? Give highlights from its history.

_____

_____

_____

_____

8. Compare your findings with classmates. What examples of humor did you and other students find? List authors, titles, and humor types in the chart below.

| Author | Title | Humor Type |
|--------|-------|------------|
|        |       |            |
|        |       |            |
|        |       |            |
|        |       |            |
|        |       |            |
|        |       |            |
|        |       |            |
|        |       |            |
|        |       |            |

# Comic Literature

## Off You Go

## Activity 1: Lighten Up the Screen

| | |
|---|---|
| **Goal:** | To analyze humor in a favorite movie or television show |
| **Materials:** | television/DVD player |

## Directions

Go watch television! Choose any film or television show that you find funny. Analyze the comedic elements of one scene or the show as a whole. Answer the questions below.

Film/show title: _____

Brief overview (summarize the plot):

_____

_____

1. What's so funny? Describe the scene below.

   _____

   _____

   _____

   _____

2. What is the structure of the comedy? What is the situation? How is it set up? How does it unfold or resolve?

   _____

   _____

   _____

   _____

   _____

   _____

   _____

   _____

# Comic Literature
## Off You Go

3. What forms of humor are used? Give specific examples.

_____

_____

_____

_____

_____

_____

_____

_____

_____

# Comic Literature
## Off You Go

## Activity 2: Spoofs and Goofs

| | |
|---|---|
| **Goal:** | To transform a literary character or scene using satire, parody, farce, and other forms of humor |
| **Materials:** | scene props (optional) |
| **Tools:** | Comedic Scene Feedback Form |

Shift your sense of humor into high gear and develop a comedic scene inspired by a literary work or character you studied in class. Your scene can be a satire, a parody, a farce, or a combination of these elements.

**Comedic Scene Guidelines**

❏ Your scene should be 8 to 10 minutes long. You will perform it.

❏ You may choose the format: skit, sketch, stand-up routine, monologue, sitcom scene, and so forth.

❏ You must include clear evidence of at least one of the forms of literary humor studied during this project.

❏ Your final script should be neatly typed in script format. Give your scene a title, identify speakers, and provide parenthetical character, prop, or stage directions if important.

## Directions

1. Choose a character, a situation, or a theme from literature.

2. Brainstorm ideas. Which characters or situations lend themselves to a thicker layer of humor? You might try one of the following:

   - Take a funny person or situation and make that person or situation funny in a different way. Change subtle satire to outright farce.
   - Take tragedy and turn it around.
   - Give a new twist to an old plot.
   - Imagine a character doing a stand-up routine for an audience in his or her time or in ours.
   - Parody a classic idea—for example, star-crossed lovers, the quest, a hero's fall or rise, and so forth.

# Comic Literature
## Off You Go

3. Imagine the scene. Run through it in your head. Take notes. Draw pictures if that helps.

4. Improvise the scene. Try different elements or twists until you like what you have. Write down the basic ideas and flow in an informal outline or sequential list. Capture lines if you can, especially funny ones, but don't stress over every line and word spoken.

5. Write a draft on paper. Read it aloud with others. Gather feedback. Brainstorm new ideas, gags, or jokes.

6. Prepare your final script on paper. Practice the scene.

7. Perform your scene.

8. Use the Comedic Scene Feedback form to let performers know how they did.

# Comic Literature
## Expedition Tool

## Comedic Scene Feedback Form

Scene title: _____

Performers: _____

What was the funniest part of the scene (by intention)? Why?

_____
_____
_____
_____

What forms of humor were used in the scene? Give specific examples.

_____
_____
_____
_____

What worked well? Why?

_____
_____
_____
_____

What might the writers and/or performers change to improve the scene? Why?

_____
_____
_____
_____

*Expeditions in Your Classroom: English Language Arts*

# Comic Literature

## Expedition Tool

How would you rate these elements overall?

|  | Poor | Okay | Good | Wow! |
|---|---|---|---|---|
| Presentation/delivery | 1 | 2 | 3 | 4 |
| Creativity/scene idea | 1 | 2 | 3 | 4 |
| Use of humor elements | 1 | 2 | 3 | 4 |

List any other constructive comments or feedback below.

_____

_____

_____

_____

_____

_____

_____

# Comic Literature

## Check Yourself!

### Skill Check

1. What are important ingredients of comedic delivery? _____

   _____

   _____

2. Explain the difference between satire and parody. Provide examples from literature to
   support your points.

   _____

   _____

   _____

   _____

   _____

   _____

3. People have said the following about humor and comedy. Choose one quotation and
   respond to it on another sheet of paper. What does the person mean? Do you agree
   or disagree? Explain your answer.

   > Humor can be dissected as a frog can, but the thing dies in the process
   > and the innards are discouraging to any but the pure scientific mind.
   >
   > —E. B. White

   > Humor is the only test of gravity, and gravity of humor; for a subject
   > which will not bear raillery is suspicious, and a jest which will not bear
   > serious examination is false wit.
   >
   > —Aristotle

   > Humor is also a way of saying something serious.
   >
   > —T. S. Eliot

   > Comedy is nothing more than tragedy deferred.
   >
   > —Pico Iyer

   > Humor is a rubber sword—it allows you to make a point without
   > drawing blood.
   >
   > —Mary Hirsch

# Comic Literature
## Check Yourself!

### Self-Assessment and Reflection
**Project Management**

**Before You Go**

- ❑ I can identify different forms of literary humor and give examples.
- ❑ I'm honestly not sure I understand forms of literary humor and have asked my teacher for additional help.

**Off You Go**

- ❑ I reviewed the project challenge and project materials carefully and thoroughly. I understand the requirements: humor research, the analysis of a show or a movie, and the development and performance of a comedic scene and its script.
- ❑ I researched my group's form of humor and found a great example of its use in literature.
- ❑ My analysis of a television show or movie scene is complete and insightful.
- ❑ I contributed significantly to my team's comedic scene idea and the development of the script. I helped write parts of the script.
- ❑ We read a draft of our script aloud and used the opportunity to improve it.
- ❑ Our final performance was well-organized. We practiced the scene and were prepared to perform it.
- ❑ Our final script is neatly typed in script format and contains no errors in grammar, spelling, or punctuation.

**Do You Know?**

- ❑ I can define the Lingo to Learn vocabulary terms for this project and give an example of each.
- ❑ I completed the Skill Check questions and carefully reviewed questions I answered incorrectly.

# Comic Literature
## Check Yourself!

**Reflection**

1. What were the most challenging aspects of this project for you and why?

   _____

   _____

   _____

   _____

   _____

   _____

   _____

2. What skills did this project help you develop?

   _____

   _____

   _____

   _____

   _____

   _____

   _____

3. If you did this project again, what might you do differently and why?

   _____

   _____

   _____

   _____

   _____

   _____

   _____

# ☉n Air

## ☉verview
Students research and analyze talk radio terminology, scriptwriting, tone, style, and presentation. Then they write their own short radio program pilot.

## Time
Total time: 8 to 12 hours

- Before You Go—Radio Speak: 30 minutes
- Before You Go—Tuning In: one 55-minute class or 30 to 60 minutes of homework, plus a 30-minute class discussion
- Activity—Sound Stories: three 55-minute class periods and 4 to 6 hours of homework

## Skill Focus
- analyzing story/presentation structure
- evaluating media content
- writing skills
- oral-presentation skills
- using technology

## Prior Knowledge
story structure

## Team Formation
Students work individually or in groups of two to three students.

## Lingo to Learn—Terms to Know
- **hook:** in radio, the catchy part of the song that listeners remember and like the most
- **sound bite:** snippet of an interview used in a news story (usually 5 to 15 seconds long)

## Suggested Steps
### Preparation

- Arrange time and equipment for students to use computers and the Internet.
- If available, arrange for the use of school recording and audio-editing equipment.
- If listening to a program as a class, use the web resources to find a good selection.
- Consider how students will be grouped together.

# On Air

## Day 1

1. Provide an overview of the project and review project materials.

2. Assign Before You Go: Radio Speak. This requires Internet access.

**Homework**

Have students research and learn radio terminology.

## Day 2

1. Review terminology. Ask if students are familiar with any of the words.

2. Introduce Before You Go: Tuning In.

3. Assign students to find and analyze a radio program. Direct them to project web sites for options. Alternatively, select one program and listen together. Try "Our Favorite Shows" from *This American Life* or something from Youth Radio.

4. Discuss program elements, presenter techniques, and the art of writing for radio. Assign an additional show for homework if desired. *Optional:* Review and discuss the comic book *Radio: An Illustrated Guide* by Jessica Abel and Ira Glass. (See Other Helpful Resources for additional ideas.)

**Homework**

Have students analyze a radio program if they have not done so in class. They can also read articles on writing for radio. See Other Helpful Resources.

## Day 3

1. Review the activity Sound Stories (final product) and show guidelines.

2. Assign due dates for the concept overview, draft script, final script, recording, and program teaser.

3. Divide students into groups.

4. Provide recording instructions (address final format, where students record if at school, and so forth).

5. Give students time to brainstorm ideas.

# ☉n Air

**Day 4**

1. Review concept overviews. Students can present them for class feedback or give them to you to review.

2. Approve concepts or ask for additional information.

3. Provide students with time to work.

**Day 5 through Script Draft Due Date**

1. Check progress.

2. Ask students about program changes and script progress. Review drafts if needed.

3. Schedule and supervise recording sessions if needed.

**Final Script and Recording Due Date**

1. Introduce the Listener Feedback Survey. Model appropriate responses and feedback.

2. Play recordings. Ask students to use the Listener Feedback Survey to evaluate one another.

3. Have students read their teasers in between shows.

4. Collect final scripts.

**Final Day**

1. Have students complete the Check Yourself! Skill Check worksheet.

2. Check and review answers.

3. Have students complete the Check Yourself! Self-Assessment and Reflection worksheet and submit it (optional).

## Project Management Tips and Notes

- If using school equipment, build in extra time to instruct students on how to record and edit audio files. Specify the final output (for instance, an MP3 file burned to disk that they will give you).
- Consider using podcast technology.
- If technology isn't available, do not record students. Instead, have them read their work aloud.

# On Air

## Suggested Assessment

Use the English Language Arts Project Assessment Rubric or the following point system:

| | |
|---|---|
| Team and class participation | 15 points |
| Before You Go: Radio Speak | 5 points |
| Before You Go: Tuning In | 10 points |
| Program script | 40 points |
| Program recording | 20 points |
| Program teaser | 5 points |
| Self-Assessment and Reflection | 5 points |

## Extension Activities

- Have students write a business letter to the program director of a local talk radio station pitching their program idea. Look at actual pitch submission guidelines.
- Have students research how they might create a class or school radio station and/or create podcasts.

## NCTE/IRA Standards Connection

4. Students adjust their use of spoken, written, and visual language (e.g., conventions, style, vocabulary) to communicate effectively with a variety of audiences and for different purposes.

5. Students employ a wide range of strategies as they write and use different writing process elements appropriately to communicate with different audiences for a variety of purposes.

6. Students apply knowledge of language structure, language conventions (e.g., spelling and punctuation), media techniques, figurative language, and genre to create, critique, and discuss print and non-print texts.

8. Students use a variety of technological and information resources (e.g., libraries, databases, computer networks, video) to gather and synthesize information and to create and communicate knowledge.

11. Students participate as knowledgeable, reflective, creative, and critical members of a variety of literacy communities.

12. Students use spoken, written, and visual language to accomplish their own purposes (e.g., for learning, enjoyment, persuasion, and the exchange of information).

# ☉n Air

## Other Helpful Resources

- About.com: Radio Glossary
  http://radio.about.com/library/blglossary.htm?PM=ss12_radio

- The Association of Independents in Radio: Radio College (Ask the Expert: Pitches that Work)
  www.airmedia.org/PageInfo.php?PageID=236

- The Association of Independents in Radio: Radio College (Submission Guidelines for Pitching Stories to Radio)
  www.airmedia.org/PageInfo.php?PageID=266

- Current.org: Mo' better radio (an interview with Ira Glass)
  (You may want to review this resource first to make sure content is appropriate for your students.)
  www.current.org/people/p809i1.html

- This American Life
  www.thisamericanlife.com
  Under "For educators," look for the comic book *Radio: An Illustrated Guide* for information on how to find and write for radio. You can order the book for $5; sneak previews are also available on the site.

## Answer Key
### Before You Go: Radio Speak

1. the part of the song that the listener is most likely to remember (the catchy part)

2. Deejay term for when to stop talking as a song starts; you can talk during the instrumental lead-in but should not "step" on the beginning of the vocals.

3. Listeners who actually participate—they call in to ask questions, suggest songs, or enter contests (versus passives who do not participate).

4. place where commercials are typically played during a broadcast hour

5. to copy a piece of audio

6. very short snippet of audio from an interview (also called an "actuality")

7. when a deejay introduces a song as it begins playing or states the name of the radio station (call letters) and then introduces the song (versus a back sell in which the deejay gives the information after the song)

8. starting another audio element too soon so that two audio tracks play at the same time

9. the number of people who listened to a station during a given time period, given as a percent of all radio listeners for that time period

10. too many commercials or non-program elements right after another

11. Answers will vary.

### Check Yourself! Skill Check

1. Both require you to have a good sense of story line and story structure. You need to hook your audience the same way the opening pages of a book or the first scene of a movie tries to hook an audience. Both a radio broadcast and a story have a logic or plot and often require character development. They might introduce a problem or a complication, or a protagonist and an antagonist (two sides of an issue). Radio programs are produced; much thought goes into outlining what will be covered, editing the material, and piecing together the best elements for an engaging program.

2. In radio writing, the writer must paint clear mental pictures—including details that enable listeners to "see" and feel what is going on. The writer must also be very conscious of clarity, time, and pace. He or she knows the listener won't go back and listen again so points must be clear, well-organized, and delivered in a way that maintains the listener's attention.

# ☉n Air

## Expedition ☉verview

### Challenge

A local radio station is looking for fresh stories and programs for its talk-radio format, and you are brimming with ideas! But do you have what it takes to write for radio? In this project, you will brush up on radio speak and explore the craft of writing in a medium that requires you to be the eyes of your audience. You will then write and record your own short talk-radio program.

### ☉bjectives

- To analyze talk-radio programming and learn radio writing techniques
- To compare and contrast writing for talk radio with writing for other purposes
- To apply your writing and oral-presentation skills

### Project Activities

**Before You Go**
- Radio Speak
- Tuning In

**Off You Go**
- Activity: Sound Stories

### Expedition Tools

- Program Concept and Teaser
- Listener Feedback Survey

### ☉ther Materials Needed

- voice recorder (cassette recorder, MP3 player, computer, and so forth)
- computer with Internet access and sound-editing ability (or two voice recorders)

### Lingo to Learn–Terms to Know

- hook
- sound bite

### Helpful Web Resources

- About.com: How to Create Your Own Radio Show
  http://radio.about.com/od/createyourownradioshow/How_to_Create_Your_Own_Radio_Show.htm

# On Air

## Expedition Overview

- About.com: Radio Glossary
  http://radio.about.com/library/blglossary.htm?PM=ss12_radio

- American Museum of Radio
  www.americanradiomuseum.org

- The Association of Independents in Radio: Radio College
  www.airmedia.org/PageInfo.php?PageID=3

- Community-Media.com: Writing for Radio—The Basics
  www.community-media.com/writing.html

- The Generic Radio Workshop: Vintage Radio Script Library
  www.genericradio.com

- National Geographic: Pulse of the Planet
  http://pulseplanet.nationalgeographic.com

- National Public Radio: Radio Diaries—Teenage Diaries
  www.radiodiaries.org/teenagediaries.html

- Sound Portraits
  www.soundportraits.org

- Sound Portraits: Record Your Own Radio Documentary
  http://soundportraits.org/education/how_to_record

- Youth Radio
  www.youthradio.org

# On Air

## Before You Go

## Radio Speak

| | |
|---|---|
| **Goal:** | To research and learn common radio terminology |
| **Materials:** | computer with Internet access |

## Directions

Write the definition for each of the following radio terms below in your own words.

1. hook: _____

2. hit the post: _____

3. actives: _____

4. stop set: _____

5. dub: _____

6. sound bite: _____

7. front sell: _____

8. miscue: _____

9. share: _____

10. clutter: _____

11. one additional term of interest to you: _____

_____

# On Air

## Before You Go

## Tuning In

| | |
|---|---|
| **Goal:** | To analyze and critique elements of a short talk-radio program |
| **Materials:** | computer with Internet access; the ability to listen to an online radio broadcast |

## Directions

Listen to a short talk-radio program online. Analyze it using the following questions as a guide. Your teacher will provide a link to a specific radio program or allow you to select one.

1. What is the program about?

_____

_____

_____

_____

_____

2. Can you detect any structure in the program?

_____

_____

_____

_____

_____

3. What techniques does the host or interviewer use to draw in the listener?

_____

_____

_____

_____

_____

©2007 Walch Publishing

# On Air

## Before You Go

4. What techniques does the program use to give listeners mental pictures, visual clues, or references?

_____

_____

_____

_____

_____

5. What techniques are used to maintain pace and interest in the topic?

_____

_____

_____

_____

_____

6. Does the program make any big statement? If so, how is the point made?

_____

_____

_____

_____

_____

7. What other observations can you make about the program?

_____

_____

_____

_____

_____

# On Air

## Off You Go

### Activity: Sound Stories

> **Goal:** To develop, script, and record a talk-radio program
>
> **Materials:** recording equipment or computer with audio/audio-editing capability; one golf ball per group; graph paper; masking tape; pencils

There are hundreds of variations of the talk-radio show genre—news features, radio documentaries, crime and mystery programs, music-appreciation programs, call-in shows, children's programming, radio soaps, reading selections, and more. The program director at your station is interested in anything that might attract a market.

Your job is to develop a compelling program concept. Create a pilot that highlights just how good it could be.

---

**Talk-Radio Show Guidelines**

❑ Your piece must be 10 to 15 minutes long.

❑ Your final product should include a typed script and the recorded piece.

❑ It can be a complete, self-contained piece, or it can showcase an excerpt of a longer program.

❑ You may choose any topic and format.

❑ You may include interviews, audience participation, songs, and so forth. You must still provide the "stitching" that weaves pieces of the show together—introductions, explanations, transitions, and other narrative elements.

❑ You may involve other people as characters, call-in participants, interview subjects, and so forth in the show. Their roles may be scripted (as in mock interviews) or actual footage.

❑ You may include commercials, public service announcements (PSAs), or sponsor messages.

---

# On Air

## Off You Go

### Directions

1. Brainstorm ideas. What type of show do you want? Start with the type of show, then think about topics and show format. Use your web resources to listen to program examples from youth and other radio stations.

2. Use the Program Concept and Teaser sheet to outline your idea. Your teacher will review it and give you the go-ahead to produce.

3. List the steps you need to take to pull your program together. What materials or content do you need? Do you want to interview anyone?

4. Collect your material. Don't forget to take notes—even if you use a recorder! Good radio journalists fill in details listeners can't see.

5. Create a draft of your script. Remember, your show is like a good story, no matter what topic or format you choose. It should have structure, flow, and logic. What will you open with? What will you close with? What context does your listener need to hook into or visualize the topic?

   Your script should be typed and should include the program title, genre, and recommended time slot. Use typical script format. Identify the speaker and what he or she says. Include interview sound bites or excerpts, call-in character comments, narration, and so forth. If you create a music show, include the song title, artist, length of the song, and a description or synopsis if not provided in the song intro. If needed, look at sample scripts or transcripts provided on the radio program sites listed in your web resources.

6. Read the script aloud. Does it flow? Does it sound natural? Is it within the time limit? Get feedback from other students and/or family members.

7. Record your final program. Follow any recording format instructions provided by your teacher.

8. Write a one-paragraph teaser for your show that the program director and marketing department can use to advertise.

9. Go live! Play the shows in class and review them. Use the Listener Feedback Survey to provide feedback notes to each show's producer. You might interject "teasers" to generate excitement for upcoming shows.

# On Air

## Expedition Tool

### Program Concept and Teaser

Producer name: _____

Write a short overview of your program idea. Make sure to describe the type and format of your program. Who is your audience? What topic will your program cover that will be attractive to your audience? What will it take to produce the program (interviews, song examples, story development, and so forth)?

_____

_____

_____

_____

_____

_____

_____

_____

_____

_____

_____

_____

Once you complete your show, write the text for a short, compelling teaser the station can use to attract an audience to your show.

_____

_____

_____

_____

_____

# On Air

## Expedition Tool

### Listener Feedback Survey

Listener name: _____

Name of show: _____

Producer: _____


Did you like the broadcast? What did you like most? least? Explain.

_____

_____

_____

_____


Was anything particularly effective? not effective? Explain.

_____

_____

_____

_____


How would you rate these elements of the piece?

|  | Poor | Okay | Good | Wow! |
|---|---|---|---|---|
| Entertainment/interest value: | 1 | 2 | 3 | 4 |
| Logic, organization, and flow: | 1 | 2 | 3 | 4 |
| Overall production quality: | 1 | 2 | 3 | 4 |


Do you have any recommendations? Explain.

_____

_____

_____

_____

# On Air

## Check Yourself!

### Skill Check

1.  In what ways is a radio broadcast like a story? What skills do you need for both? Explain.

_____

_____

_____

_____

_____

_____

_____

_____

_____

_____

_____

_____

_____

2.  Why might writing for radio improve writing skills overall? How has it helped you?

_____

_____

_____

_____

_____

_____

_____

_____

_____

_____

_____

# On Air

## Check Yourself!

### Self-Assessment and Reflection
**Project Management**

**Before You Go**

- ❏ I understand the basic elements and structure of a radio program.
- ❏ I can compare and contrast radio writing with other forms of writing (television, narrative, and so forth).
- ❏ I'm honestly not sure I understand the writing skills I need for this project and have asked my teacher for additional help.

**Off You Go**

- ❏ I reviewed the project challenge and project materials carefully and thoroughly. I understand the products I will produce: radio terminology definitions, a radio program analysis, the script for a short radio program, a recording of the program, and a program teaser.
- ❏ My Radio Speak worksheet is complete and gives definitions in my own words. (I did not copy them verbatim from the site.)
- ❏ My radio program analysis is complete and thoughtful. I listened carefully for techniques and structure clues.
- ❏ I provided a clear and complete view of my radio program idea on my Program Concept and Teaser worksheet.
- ❏ I managed my work effectively. I had a plan for how to develop my program and script, and I followed it.
- ❏ My final script includes all required information and is typed in script format.
- ❏ My program teaser is concise, well-written, and attention-grabbing.
- ❏ My recording is audible and showcases my best speaking skills.
- ❏ I reviewed peer feedback on my radio program and provided feedback to others.

**Do You Know?**

- ❏ I can define the Lingo to Learn vocabulary terms for this project and give an example of each.
- ❏ I completed the Skill Check questions and carefully reviewed questions I answered incorrectly.

# ☉n Air
## Check Yourself!

### Reflection

1. What were the most challenging aspects of this project for you and why?

   _____

   _____

   _____

   _____

   _____

   _____

   _____

2. What skills did this project help you develop?

   _____

   _____

   _____

   _____

   _____

   _____

   _____

3. If you did this project again, what might you do differently and why?

   _____

   _____

   _____

   _____

   _____

   _____

   _____

# Junior Scientist Magazine

## Overview

Students learn about writing magazine articles and then consider what they know about writing for a specific audience to write a feature article for a children's science magazine.

## Time

Total time: 7 to 8 hours

- Before You Go—What's in a Feature?: one 55-minute class and/or homework

- Activity—Journalism for Juniors: six to seven 55-minute class periods and/or homework assignments

## Skill Focus
- compare and contrast
- research
- critical thinking
- writing

## Prior Knowledge

Some familiarity with styles of news articles will be helpful.

## Team Formation

Students work individually on this project.

## Lingo to Learn—Terms to Know
- **angle:** slant or viewpoint from which a story is told
- **feature article:** a more in-depth look at what's going on behind the news (versus a breaking story or hard news)
- **five *W*'s and *H*:** who, what, where, when, why, and how; questions that a news story should answer
- **inverted pyramid:** common style of writing news in which the most important or interesting information is presented first
- **lede/lead:** first paragraph of a news story

# Junior Scientist Magazine

## Suggested Steps

### Preparation

- Collect a sampling of magazines written for children and adults. Make sure to include a variety of science magazines.
- Contact a teacher of elementary grades to see if students there can review your students' articles.

### Day 1

1. Provide an overview of the project.

2. Review project materials.

3. Discuss the Lingo to Learn—Terms to Know. Provide examples and clarify any misconceptions. Define the following types of leads for students:

   - **blind lead:** summarizes but leaves out an essential detail in order to intrigue the reader; used in feature writing

   - **narrative lead:** tells a story, for example, from the perspective of the person featured; classic way to start a feature

   - **novelty lead:** a unique start; for example, a quotation, a question, an anecdote, or an exclamatory or declarative statement

   - **summary lead:** summarizes all important information in the article; used most for news stories

4. Explain Before You Go: What's in a Feature? Assign the activity for homework or allow students to work in the library if both print and online magazines are available there. Alternatively, divide students into groups of three or four and give each group both types of magazines to analyze in class.

### Homework

Have students complete magazine article analysis.

### Day 2

1. Discuss magazine article analysis. Show examples.

2. Explain the activity Journalism for Juniors (final product) and review article guidelines.

# Junior Scientist Magazine

3. Assign due dates for the draft and final article. Indicate whether students will work in class, at home, or elsewhere.

4. Discuss ways students might identify topics and organize their projects.

**Day 3 through Draft Due Date**

1. Check in with students to review topics, article angles, ideas, and so forth.

2. Work with students on checking sources. Encourage students to use primary sources if possible.

3. Have students trade drafts to conduct peer editing and complete the Editorial Review Form.

**Final Project Due Date**

1. Have students display their articles. Invite students to present a summary and highlights.

2. If possible, visit an elementary school class. Have students buddy up with the elementary students to share their articles.

3. Collect articles.

**Final Day**

1. Have students complete the Skill Check questions.

2. Check and review answers.

3. Have students complete the Check Yourself! Self-Assessment and Reflection worksheet and submit it (optional).

## Project Management Tips and Notes

- Have students tell you project topics once they have defined them.
- Once projects are underway, ask students to explain their science topic to the class (as practice). Discuss methods for understanding and communicating challenging material.
- Build in computer lab time at the front end of the project so that you can guide initial research (for example, address high-quality scientific sources, methods students might use to understand concepts, and so forth).
- With your students, decide in advance which is most valuable: receiving feedback from younger students on final products, or receiving feedback while articles are still in draft.

# Junior Scientist Magazine

## Suggested Assessment

Use the English Language Arts Project Assessment Rubric or the following point system:

| | |
|---|---|
| Team and class participation | 10 points |
| Before You Go: What's in a Feature? | 25 points |
| Activity: Journalism for Juniors | 60 points |
| Self-Assessment and Reflection | 5 points |

## Extension Activities

- Students can learn more about journalism skills at American Society of Newspaper Editors: High School Journalism: http://highschooljournalism.org/.
- Have students actually submit their work to a children's magazine. If this is a goal from the start, be sure to review the publication's submission guidelines.
- Compile students' articles and publish them as a class magazine.

## NCTE/IRA Standards Connection

1. Students read a wide range of print and non-print texts to build an understanding of texts, of themselves, and of the cultures of the United States and the world; to acquire new information; to respond to the needs and demands of society and the workplace; and for personal fulfillment. Among these texts are fiction and nonfiction, classic and contemporary works.

3. Students apply a wide range of strategies to comprehend, interpret, evaluate, and appreciate texts. They draw on their prior experience, their interactions with other readers and writers, their knowledge of word meaning and of other texts, their word identification strategies, and their understanding of textual features (e.g., sound-letter correspondence, sentence structure, context, graphics).

4. Students adjust their use of spoken, written, and visual language (e.g., conventions, style, vocabulary) to communicate effectively with a variety of audiences and for different purposes.

5. Students employ a wide range of strategies as they write and use different writing process elements appropriately to communicate with different audiences for a variety of purposes.

8. Students use a variety of technological and information resources (e.g., libraries, databases, computer networks, video) to gather and synthesize information and to create and communicate knowledge.

# Junior Scientist Magazine

## Answer Key
### Check Yourself! Skill Check

1. A news story covers "straight hard" news and current events; the style is concise and to the point. A news story often makes use of an inverted pyramid style with the most important information—often a summary of all essential information—up front in the lead paragraph. A feature article is longer and more in-depth. The writer has more time and space to develop the idea. The article doesn't have to be tied to a current event. There is more flexibility with structure, style, and content; more use of novel leads; and often the use of photographs and other elements. The overall structure of a news story and feature article is similar (writers must grab readers' attention early), and the same attention must be given to accuracy and the ethical standards of journalism.

2. Answers will vary, but lead types could include summary, blind, narrative, or novelty (quotation, question, anecdote, exclamatory or declarative statement.

3. Answers will vary but might include draw a diagram; make a concept map; reread the idea and pick out main points; say the idea aloud or try to explain it to someone else; and visualize it.

# Junior Scientist Magazine
## Expedition Overview

## Challenge
Have you heard the expression, "Keep it simple"? That is exactly the idea of this project. Your task is to take a tough, complex, or challenging science topic and write a simple-yet-engaging feature article about it for a children's magazine. Your audience? Kids, age seven to twelve years old, who know a great story when they read one!

## Objectives
- To learn the basics of journalistic writing
- To compare and contrast writing samples
- To research and write about a scientific topic
- To deconstruct a complex idea or advanced topic and present it in a clear and simple manner
- To learn how to tailor your writing style to specific audiences

## Project Activities
**Before You Go**
- What's in a Feature?

**Off You Go**
- Activity: Journalism for Juniors

## Expedition Tools
Editorial Review Form

## Other Materials Needed
- magazine articles (for various age groups and topics)
- computer with Internet access
- Other materials will vary by project (digital camera, art supplies, and so forth).

## Lingo to Learn—Terms to Know
- angle
- feature article
- five *W*'s and *H*
- inverted pyramid
- lede (or lead)

# Junior Scientist Magazine

## Expedition Overview

### Helpful Web Resources

- American Society of Newspaper Editors: High School Journalism
  http://highschooljournalism.org

- Dig: The Archeology Magazine for Kids
  www.digonsite.com

- National Geographic Kids
  http://kids.nationalgeographic.com

- The New England Journal of Medicine
  http://content.nejm.org

- Odyssey Magazine
  www.odysseymagazine.com

- Popular Science Magazine
  www.popsci.com/popsci

- Poynter Online
  www.poynter.org

- Scholastic Classroom Magazines: DynaMath
  http://teacher.scholastic.com/products/classmags/dynamath.htm

- American Association for the Advancement of Science (AAAS): Science Magazine
  www.sciencemag.org

- Science News for Kids
  www.sciencenewsforkids.org

- Scientific American: Ask the Experts
  www.sciam.com/askexpert_directory.cfm

- TeacherVision: Basic Journalism
  www.teachervision.fen.com/journalism/writing/6042.html?detoured=1

- Time Magazine for Kids
  www.timeforkids.com/TFK

# Junior Scientist Magazine

## Before You Go

## What's in a Feature?

> **Goals:** To research and review basic principles of journalism; to examine and evaluate the structure and elements of feature articles
>
> **Materials:** two magazine articles (adult/teen and children's)

## Directions

1. Find two feature articles—one from a magazine for teens or adults, the other from a children's magazine (for example, *Highlights*, *Cricket*, *Time for Kids*, *Sports Illustrated for Kids*, and so forth).

2. Read both carefully.

3. Compare and contrast the articles using the chart below.

4. Be prepared to discuss which journalistic elements each magazine uses and how it uses the elements. Consider the differences you see. Give specific details and examples.

| Article elements | Adult/teen magazine title: | Children's magazine title: |
|---|---|---|
| **Lead** (blind, narrative, novelty, summary) | | |
| **Angle** | | |
| **The five *W*'s and *H*** (who, what, where, when, why, and how) | | |
| **Inverted pyramid structure** | | |
| **Sentence complexity** (average number of words per sentence) | | |

# Junior Scientist Magazine

## Off You Go

## Activity: Journalism for Juniors

> **Goal:** To write a feature article for a children's science magazine
>
> **Tools:** Editorial Review Form

Your young readers await the next issue of their favorite magazine. You need to get your feature article written now! Choose your topic and get to work!

---

**Article Guidelines**

❑ Your article should be between 750 and 1,000 words.

❑ Choose any newsworthy topic from the fields of science, medicine, engineering, or technology.

❑ Include illustrations, sketches, or diagrams that explain the science behind the story. These may be hand-drawn and rough, but they should be accurate.

❑ You may also include fun elements to engage young readers, such as images, sidebars, word games, riddles, activity or experiment suggestions, and so forth.

❑ You must use and correctly cite at least three reputable sources. Include endnotes if appropriate.

❑ Your final article should be typed and should contain no errors in grammar, spelling, or punctuation.

---

## Directions

1. Browse children's science magazines (such as *Ranger Rick*, *Tracks*, *Your Big Backyard,* and so forth) to get a feel for article elements, styles, and topics. Visit the online magazines listed under Helpful Web Resources or visit the library for hard copies.

2. Brainstorm topics. Check out science magazines written for adults. Which topics are getting cover and feature attention? Look at sites that include features such as "ask an expert" or "ask a scientist." What questions do people ask?

3. Decide on your topic. Don't forget to think about the angle you want to cover.

# Junior Scientist Magazine

## Off You Go

4. List the elements you want to include in your article (quotations, images, activity sidebars, and so forth).

5. Perform research. Remember, you must have at least three sources. If you want, interview a scientist or an expert on your topic. Just let your teacher know you want to do this.

6. Pin down the "big idea"—the science at work. Create a mind map or a diagram, explain the idea to someone else, or model it. Do whatever it takes to get the concept organized in your mind.

7. Write a draft of your article. Try to get feedback from your target age group.

8. Exchange your article with a classmate. He or she will serve as your features editor, and you will serve as his or hers. Use the Editorial Review Form to evaluate the article.

9. Revise and finalize your article.

10. Publish your article. Share it with younger students in your community.

# Junior Scientist Magazine

## Expedition Tool

### Editorial Review Form

Article title: _____

Author: _____ Reviewer: _____

**Evaluation**

|  | Poor | Below Average | Average | Above Average |
|---|---|---|---|---|
| Interest/appeal | 1 | 2 | 3 | 4 |
| Technical quality | 1 | 2 | 3 | 4 |
| Grammar/style | 1 | 2 | 3 | 4 |
| Length | 1 | 2 | 3 | 4 |
| Overall | 1 | 2 | 3 | 4 |

Comments/critique: _____

_____

_____

**Recommendation**

❑  Accept as is or with minor revisions

  Suggestions: _____

  _____

  _____

❑  Revise and resubmit

  Revisions requested: _____

  _____

  _____

❑  Reject

  Reason for rejection: _____

  _____

  _____

# Junior Scientist Magazine
## Check Yourself!

### Skill Check

1. What is the difference between a news story and a feature article? How are they similar?

   _____

   _____

   _____

   _____

   _____

   _____

   _____

2. Using different lead types, write three leads for the "story" of your day so far.

   _____

   _____

   _____

   _____

   _____

   _____

3. What techniques or methods do you use (or could you use) to understand a complicated idea?

   _____

   _____

   _____

   _____

   _____

   _____

*Expeditions in Your Classroom: English Language Arts*                ©2007 Walch Publishing

# Junior Scientist Magazine
## Check Yourself!

### Self-Assessment and Reflection
#### Project Management

### Before You Go

- ❏ I understand the basic elements and structure of a journalistic piece.
- ❏ I can identify types of leads used in news stories and feature articles.
- ❏ I can explain the idea of the inverted pyramid structure.
- ❏ I'm honestly not sure I understand the journalistic skills I need for this project and have asked my teacher for additional help.

### Off You Go

- ❏ I reviewed the project challenge and project materials carefully and thoroughly.
- ❏ I understand the products I will produce: a comparison of magazine articles for children and adults, and a feature article for children on a challenging science topic.
- ❏ My comparison of magazine articles for children and adults is comprehensive. I carefully reviewed the elements and styles of both articles and provided details and examples that support my findings.
- ❏ I selected a challenging topic for my article. It will take work to translate it into information that a seven- to twelve-year-old can digest.
- ❏ I reviewed children's magazines to get ideas for the content and structure of my feature article.
- ❏ I used at least three reputable sources for my research.
- ❏ I can explain the science of my project clearly.
- ❏ I got feedback on my draft article from peers and/or younger children.
- ❏ My final article is typed and free of errors of fact, grammar, spelling, and punctuation.

### Do You Know?

- ❏ I can define the Lingo to Learn vocabulary terms for this project and give an example of each.
- ❏ I completed the Skill Check questions and carefully reviewed questions I answered incorrectly.

# Junior Scientist Magazine

## Check Yourself!

Reflection

1. What were the most challenging aspects of this project for you and why?

   _____

   _____

   _____

   _____

   _____

   _____

   _____

2. What skills did this project help you develop?

   _____

   _____

   _____

   _____

   _____

   _____

   _____

3. If you did this project again, what might you do differently and why?

   _____

   _____

   _____

   _____

   _____

   _____

   _____

# Feedback, Inc.

## Overview
Students take on the role of consultants by conducting qualitative research on the operation of a local business or a nonprofit organization. They collect and analyze information gathered to make a recommendation. They prepare and give a presentation on their findings.

## Time
Total time: 11 to 15 hours

- Before You Go—Interview Review: one 55-minute class

- Activity 1—Listen and Learn: two to three 55-minute classes plus 4 to 6 hours of homework/out-of-school time

- Activity 2—Review and Recommend: two to three hours of homework plus two to three 55-minute classes for presentations

## Skill Focus
- interviewing
- business communication
- analyzing, summarizing, and presenting

## Prior Knowledge
professional phone etiquette

## Team Formation
Students work in teams of two to four students.

## Lingo to Learn—Words to Know
- **closed question:** question that has a limited number of answers from which one or more answers must be chosen (for example, a multiple-choice question)
- **open question:** question that a respondent is asked to answer in his or her own words
- **qualitative research:** research that is concerned with the process (why or how); usually relies on interviews, observations, and interactions with subjects
- **quantitative research:** research based on measuring variables and studying statistical relationships between them

# Feedback, Inc.

## Suggested Steps

### Preparation

- Brief administrators on the project. Send project information to parents. Obtain permission slips as necessary.
- Contact your local Chamber of Commerce, Rotary Club, or other community business organization for assistance finding good project sites. Students may also have contacts they can use (family friends, relatives, etc.). Create a list of options if appropriate.
- Review the web sites with interviewing tips listed under Helpful Web Resources. Compile and print copies of tips to give to students.
- Prepare scenarios for Day 1 role-play.

### Day 1

1. Provide an overview of the project and review project materials.

2. Facilitate Before You Go: Interview Review. Ask students to volunteer for role-play interviews.

3. Use the following scenarios or create your own:

   - Scenario 1 (2 students): A marketing executive of a jeans company interviews a high-school student.

   - Scenario 2 (2 students): A nurse and a patient discuss a medical issue.

   - Scenario 3 (2 students): A management consultant interviews the CEO of a candy factory.

4. Define and discuss qualitative interviewing. Ask for examples of qualitative versus quantitative questions or methods. Brainstorm questions and categorize them as qualitative or quantitative. Compare "how" questions and "why" questions, "open" questions and "closed" questions, and so forth.

5. Talk about the characteristics of a good interview. Caution students to avoid pitfalls such as leading the interviewee, using nonverbal cues, and so forth.

### Homework

Ask students to review interviewing technique tips using their web resources.

# Feedback, Inc.

## Day 2

1. Review the Observation Checklist in detail.

2. Form or assign student teams if desired.

3. Begin Activity 1: Listen and Learn. Give students a list of potential project sites or provide instructions on how to identify/propose a project site.

4. Indicate if students will work in class or at home. Assign due dates for site observations, final report, and presentation.

5. Give students time to begin planning.

## Homework

Have students identify and contact businesses or nonprofit groups they plan to research. They should begin to outline potential interviewees and draft interview questions.

## Days 3 and 4 through Observation Completion

1. Review interview questions as a class. Have students revise as needed.

2. Review and role-play interview etiquette.

3. Students should conduct research and meet to share data while you check to see how calls and observations are coming along. Have students describe highlights or interesting moments in interviews and observations (for instance, which interviews worked and why).

4. Students may begin to think about final presentations.

## Observation Completion Date through Final Presentation Due Date

1. Review final presentation guidelines.

2. Provide students with time to meet in class, at the library, or in the computer lab to review findings and work on presentations.

3. If the business or organization will review student work, ask that students send the drafts (by e-mail, by fax, or in person) to their contacts with a copy of the Student Presentation Feedback Form. If e-mailing, students should copy you on the e-mail message.

4. Schedule and invite students to give their presentations.

# Feedback, Inc.

**Final Day**

1. Have students complete the Skill Check questions.

2. Check and review answers.

3. Have students complete the Check Yourself! Self-Assessment and Reflection worksheet and submit it (optional).

## Project Management Tips and Notes

- Don't panic about how to find businesses and organizations willing to host students for the project. Students often have the contacts they need and/or can help you find them. Students might also consider evaluating the school or a program within the school community.
- If you have a predefined list of opportunities, send a letter explaining the project and the role you hope the business will play. You may want to emphasize that this is a learning experience for students (a mock "consulting" exercise), so the pressure is on the students, not on the business or organization.
- Make sure students can explain the project clearly before they contact a business or an organization. Practice "first contact" situations in class. Ask students to make a list of exactly what they want or need from the business (including a way for the contact person to give feedback on the student's final report).
- Support students who might be struggling to get information by working with them on developing strategies and forms to collect site observations or interview notes.

## Suggested Assessment

Use the English Language Arts Project Assessment Rubric or the following point system:

| | |
|---|---|
| Team and class participation | 15 points |
| Planning | 20 points |
| Site observation/interviews | 20 points |
| Final presentation | 40 points |
| Self-Assessment and Reflection | 5 points |

# Feedback, Inc.

## Extension Activities

- Have students present findings to staff at the business or organization. Give each person a copy of the Student Presentation Feedback Form to complete.
- Assign students to research a hot topic related to the business or organization observed (for example, trends in customer service, marketing, non-profit management, and so forth). Have students prepare a short brief (one to two pages long). Share the brief with the organization.

## NCTE/IRA Standards Connection

1. Students read a wide range of print and non-print texts to build an understanding of texts, of themselves, and of the cultures of the United States and the world; to acquire new information; to respond to the needs and demands of society and the workplace; and for personal fulfillment. Among these texts are fiction and nonfiction, classic and contemporary works.

4. Students adjust their use of spoken, written, and visual language (e.g., conventions, style, vocabulary) to communicate effectively with a variety of audiences and for different purposes.

5. Students employ a wide range of strategies as they write and use different writing process elements appropriately to communicate with different audiences for a variety of purposes.

7. Students conduct research on issues and interests by generating ideas and questions, and by posing problems. They gather, evaluate, and synthesize data from a variety of sources (e.g., print and non-print texts, artifacts, people) to communicate their discoveries in ways that suit their purpose and audience.

11. Students participate as knowledgeable, reflective, creative, and critical members of a variety of literacy communities.

# Feedback, Inc.

## Answer Key
### Check Yourself! Skill Check

1. Possibilities include asking "why" questions instead of "how" questions (opinion versus fact, rationale versus process); leading the interviewee; using too many closed questions instead of open questions; asking questions that are too personal before building rapport; not remaining neutral or not balancing neutrality and empathy; forgetting that the interviewee may have an agenda or may be leading the interviewer; rushing, or proceeding too slowly with uncomfortable pauses; not asking if the interviewee thinks the interviewer has left anything out.

2. Qualitative research looks at why or how; quantitative research deals with numbers or anything measurable (what, how much, where, or when). An open-ended question in a customer interview or survey is a qualitative method. A question that asks the customer to rank something or give a number is quantitative.

3. Creating a presentation is similar to writing a business letter. Make sure information is concise, clear, readable, and direct; provide only the information needed; use active voice and action verbs; and avoid fancy fonts and writing styles.

# Feedback, Inc.

## Expedition Overview

### Challenge
Feedback, Inc.—the name of your company says it all. You are good at collecting and analyzing feedback, and there is a business or an organization in your community that can use your skills. For this project, you will visit a local business or an organization, interview staff and clients, and present your findings.

### Objectives
- To learn how to collect information by conducting a qualitative interview
- To analyze and summarize key points from interviews
- To present findings in a clear, compelling, and professional manner

### Project Activities
**Before You Go**
- Interview Review

**Off You Go**
- Activity 1: Journalism for Juniors
- Activity 2: Review and Recommend

### Expedition Tools
- Observation Checklist
- Student Presentation Feedback Form

### Other Materials Needed
- computer with slide presentation software and Internet access
- voice recorder (optional)

### Lingo to Learn—Terms to Know
- closed question
- open question
- qualitative research
- quantitative research

# Feedback, Inc.

## Expedition Overview

### Helpful Web Resources

- Customer Service Manager
  www.customerservicemanager.com

- Media Bistro: Mobile Media News—On Interviewing
  www.mediabistro.com/articles/cache/a1450.asp

- Purdue University Writing Lab—Field Research: Conducting an Interview (PowerPoint)
  http://owl.english.purdue.edu/workshops/pp/interviewing.ppt

- University of Florida: College of Liberal Arts and Sciences—Qualitative Interviewing
  http://web.clas.ufl.edu/users/ardelt/Aging/QualInt.htm

# Feedback, Inc.

## Before You Go

## Interview Review

> **Goals:** To learn how interviews are used in qualitative research; to practice interviewing skills

## Directions

1. Your teacher will ask students in the class to participate in a series of imaginative interviews. Don't be afraid to volunteer!

2. Listen to each interview and try to identify what makes it work or not work. What patterns do you see? Write your notes below.

Scenario 1: _____

_____

_____

_____

Scenario 2: _____

_____

_____

_____

Scenario 3: _____

_____

_____

_____

3. Next, form a group of three students. Practice interviewing one another. One person should be the interviewer, one should be the interviewee, and the third person should be an observer.

4. Choose a topic that the interviewee knows something about. Rotate roles so that each student has an opportunity to interview. In each case, the observer should provide feedback on interview pluses and minuses.

# Feedback, Inc.
## Off You Go

## Activity 1: Listen and Learn

> | **Goal:** | To research a business or a nonprofit organization in your community |
> | --- | --- |
> | **Tools:** | Observation Checklist |
> | **Materials:** | notebook, digital camera, and voice recorder (optional) |

## Directions

1. Identify the business or nonprofit organization you want to study, or choose from options your teacher provides.

2. Conduct initial research to learn more about the business. If the business has a web site, visit it. If not, learn about the type of organization it is. Find out the following:

   - Where is the business located?
   - What service does it provide?
   - Is it part of a larger organization or network?
   - How long has it been in the community?

3. Identify the people you want to interview or the positions you might survey while on-site.

4. Prepare a list of questions to ask each group (customers, managers, and so forth). In the end, it may not be necessary or appropriate to ask every question, but write them down anyway. Type your list of questions so that your teacher can review them. You will also send a copy to the owner or manager of the business so he or she knows what to expect.

5. Contact the owner, manager, or director of your organization. Review the details of your project, the types of people you would like to interview, and the questions you would like to ask.

   Be sure to thank the contact person for giving you the opportunity to study his or her business. In addition, find out the following:

   - if he or she can give you a tour of the business to introduce you to it
   - if you can take pictures and/or record interviews.
   - if you should dress a certain way while on-site (In general, treat your visit as a professional encounter worthy of appropriate business wear.)
   - if you should focus on a particular aspect of the business (for example, how customers like the new breakfast menu)

# Feedback, Inc.

## Off You Go

- if there are any "don'ts" related to the project (don't ask this, don't disrupt a sale, etc.)
- if he or she prefers to present you when you speak with customers or staff

6. Outline the best plan for collecting the information you need. For example, you might interview some people by phone. You might speak to others during a visit to the site. For customers, you may want to create a brief survey. Determine team member assignments: How will you organize during your site visit? Who will interview whom?

7. Conduct your site visit and interview calls. Take pictures and copious notes!

8. Collect examples of materials (for example, a company brochure, a newsletter, an advertisement, or another marketing piece).

# Feedback, Inc.
## Expedition Tool

### Observation Checklist
#### Preparation

- ❑ Submit your project permission slip.
- ❑ Choose an organization and conduct preliminary research.
- ❑ Create a preliminary list of interview questions.
- ❑ Call your main contact person to outline interview and visit plans.

#### Observation and Interviews

- ❑ Decide team member assignments.
- ❑ Schedule visits and calls.
- ❑ Prepare surveys (optional).
- ❑ Conduct visit and interviews. Take notes and collect materials (a company brochure, a newsletter, an advertisement, etc.) Keep track of the people you interviewed.
- ❑ Send a thank-you note to the contact person.

#### Presentation

- ❑ With your team, review main findings from visit and interviews.
- ❑ Conduct more research if needed.
- ❑ Prepare your presentation outline.
- ❑ Create a draft of the presentation.
- ❑ Ask your main contact person to provide feedback on the draft presentation.
- ❑ Create your final presentation.
- ❑ Present to the class.
- ❑ If appropriate, present your findings and recommendations to organization staff.

### People Interviewed

| Name | Title/role | Interviewers | Date interviewed |
|------|-----------|-------------|------------------|
|      |           |             |                  |
|      |           |             |                  |
|      |           |             |                  |
|      |           |             |                  |
|      |           |             |                  |
|      |           |             |                  |
|      |           |             |                  |
|      |           |             |                  |

# Feedback, Inc.
## Off You Go

## Activity 2: Review and Recommend

| | |
|---|---|
| **Goals:** | To analyze your findings; to create a presentation to share your recommendations |
| **Materials:** | computer with slide presentation software and Internet access |

It's time for you to make sense of the information you collected and to present your findings. Your client is eager to know what you think!

**Presentation Guidelines**

Create a presentation that includes the following:

❑ the name of the organization and an overview of what it does

❑ team member names (first names only) and/or team name

❑ an overview of your research methods (who you interviewed, how many people you surveyed, where and what you observed, etc.)

❑ a summary of your findings

❑ your feedback or recommendations

❑ a closing "thank-you" slide

Your final presentation should be:

❑ well-organized and professional (You may be creative; however, too much fancy formatting and slide-show wizardry may work against you. Your presentation will be reviewed in print and as a slide show.)

❑ free of errors in spelling, punctuation, and grammar

# Feedback, Inc.

## Off You Go

### Directions

1. Meet with your team members to compare notes and findings. Have one person record a list of key points. What conclusions can you draw? Don't forget to give an example or a quotation that supports each point.

2. Identify what feedback you will provide and what recommendations you will make. Given what you heard, what do you think the business or organization does well? What should the business keep doing and why? What areas need improvement? What might the business do differently? Did customers affirm a particular product or service or have ideas for others?

   If you wish, conduct additional research to see how other businesses have handled a particular suggestion or issue.

3. Create a draft of your presentation. Review it carefully as a team—you need to be able to stand behind your work.

4. Send a copy of your draft to the main contact person at your business or organization. Include a copy of the Student Presentation Feedback Form. Ask for feedback. The contact person can return the form or provide feedback by phone—whichever is easiest for him or her.

5. If appropriate, schedule time to present your feedback to staff or see if the contact person can collect reactions.

6. Revise your presentation if needed. Present the final version in class.

# Feedback, Inc.
## Expedition Tool

### Student Presentation Feedback Form

Business or organization name: _____

Contact person name: _____

Thank you for allowing us to visit your site. Attached, please find a draft copy of our presentation. Please review it and provide feedback. This will help us to revise our work for our final presentation. Thank you!

What is your general reaction to the presentation?

_____

_____

_____

_____

_____

_____

_____

_____

How would you rate these elements?

|  | Poor | Below Average | Average | Above Average |
|---|---|---|---|---|
| Organization | 1 | 2 | 3 | 4 |
| Clarity | 1 | 2 | 3 | 4 |
| Thoughtfulness of findings/recommendations | 1 | 2 | 3 | 4 |

# Feedback, Inc.

## Expedition Tool

What are some effective points we make in our presentation?

_____

_____

_____

_____

_____

_____

What could be improved upon to make our presentation better?

_____

_____

_____

_____

_____

_____

Please include any additional comments below.

_____

_____

_____

_____

_____

_____

Please return form to:

Name: _____

E-mail or fax: _____

# Feedback, Inc.
## Check Yourself!

### Skill Check

1. What are some common mistakes an interviewer might make? Discuss at least four mistakes.

   _____

   _____

   _____

   _____

   _____

   _____

2. What is qualitative research? What is quantitative research? Give an example of both.

   _____

   _____

   _____

   _____

   _____

   _____

3. What are two or three key things to remember about creating a presentation for a business?

   _____

   _____

   _____

   _____

   _____

   _____

# Feedback, Inc.
## Check Yourself!

### Self-Assessment and Reflection
**Project Management**

**Before You Go**

- ❏ I understand the concept of qualitative interview.
- ❏ I can give examples of techniques interviewers might use or avoid.
- ❏ I'm honestly not sure I understand qualitative interview techniques and have asked my teacher for additional help.

**Off You Go**

- ❏ I reviewed the project challenge and project materials carefully and thoroughly. I understand the requirements: on-site observation and interviews and a final presentation of findings.
- ❏ My team was fully prepared to contact our project site. I can explain the project and outline what we hoped to accomplish on-site.
- ❏ My team conducted a highly professional call with our host contact person. We discussed the project, asked specifically about do's and don'ts, and outlined a clear plan for interviews and site visits.
- ❏ My team has a copy of legible notes from each interview and visit.
- ❏ Team members participated equally in planning and carrying out interviews and site visits.
- ❏ My team discussed findings together. We each contributed to the analysis and recommendations.
- ❏ Our final presentation is well-organized, error-free, and looks professional. Each team member played a substantive role in creating the presentation. We were able to send the presentation to our site contact for feedback.

**Do You Know?**

- ❏ I can define the Lingo to Learn vocabulary terms for this project and give an example of each.
- ❏ I completed the Skill Check questions and carefully reviewed questions I answered incorrectly.

# Feedback, Inc.

## Check Yourself!

### Reflection

1. What were the most challenging aspects of this project for you and why?

_____

_____

_____

_____

_____

_____

_____

2. What skills did this project help you develop?

_____

_____

_____

_____

_____

_____

_____

3. If you did this project again, what might you do differently and why?

_____

_____

_____

_____

_____

_____

_____

# The Perfect Pitch

## Overview
Students develop an idea for a box office hit or bomb and write the story specs, logline, synopsis, and query letter they need to pitch it.

## Time
Total time: 8 to 12 hours

- Before You Go—Making Every Word Count: one 30- to 55-minute class or homework assignment

- Activity 1—Story Specs: 4 to 6 hours of homework

- Activity 2—The Pitch: 2 to 4 hours of homework plus two 55-minute classes

## Skill Focus
- creative and persuasive writing
- summarizing
- grammar

## Prior Knowledge
- identifying main idea and details
- story development
- character development
- some familiarity with persuasion

## Team Formation
Students can work individually or in pairs.

## Lingo to Learn—Terms to Know
- **antagonist:** person or force that opposes the protagonist in a literary work
- **logline:** one or two sentences that describe the basic premise of a show or movie idea
- **pitch:** basic premise of a movie told in a succinct way to entice the listener into buying or supporting the work
- **protagonist:** hero or central character in a literary work
- **synopsis:** summary of a screenplay usually told in present tense

# The Perfect Pitch

## Suggested Steps

### Preparation

- Collect examples of movie loglines and synopses. Print them from newspaper or online movie listings and descriptions.
- Print one or two sample "first pages" from a movie script or screenplay.

### Day 1

1. Provide an overview of the project and review project materials.

2. Explain the term *logline* and give one or two examples.

3. Assign Before You Go: Making Every Word Count. Students may work in pairs or individually. Discuss responses.

4. Explain Activity 1: Story Specs. You might also show screenplay first pages. Discuss approach and format.

5. Form teams if desired. Review the first four pieces of written work students produce. Note that students do not complete all parts of Activity 1 at this time (synopsis and logline come later).

6. Assign due dates for movie overview, conflict and character descriptions, and first page of script.

### Homework

Have students develop movie ideas and begin Activity 1: Story Specs.

### Day 2 through First Script Page Due Date

1. Have students share their story specs in class and read first pages.

2. Discuss pros and cons of story specs. Are students' presentations of movie ideas, characters, and opening scenes attention-grabbers? Did students meet the challenge of creating concise and descriptive language?

3. Assign Activity 2: The Pitch.

4. Share examples of well-written synopses or query letters. Ask students to review tips (see Helpful Web Resources).

# The Perfect Pitch

**Homework**

Have students work on pitch materials.

**Pitch Material Due Date**

1. Invite students to pitch their movies in a fun role-play.

2. Suggest scenarios for where the pitch takes place. Alternatively, write them on slips of paper and have students choose. Have other students role-play as needed. Examples:

   • You bump into a famous movie producer in an elevator. You won't be in the elevator together for very long! You have two minutes to pitch your idea.
   • You have scheduled a lunch appointment with a movie executive.
   • You have been asked to present your idea in a meeting.
   • You run into a movie executive in the dentist's office.

3. Have students read their query letters. Critique style and quality of pitch. Compare and contrast initial movie overviews and final synopses.

4. Collect Activity 1: Story Specs, script pages, and query letters.

**Final Day**

1. Have students complete the Skill Check questions.

2. Check and review answers.

3. Have students complete the Check Yourself! Self-Assessment and Reflection worksheet and submit it (optional).

## Project Management Tips and Notes

• If students work individually, allow them to brainstorm ideas and get feedback on story specs from other students.
• Run a mock script competition and award "best idea," "best characterization," and "best first page." Have students judge. You might have them use an actual criteria sheet (for example, the 20/20 Screenwriting Competition Criteria Sheet found at http://lets-do-lunch.com/contestcriteria.pdf).

# The Perfect Pitch

## Suggested Assessment

Use the English Language Arts Project Assessment Rubric or the following point system:

| | |
|---|---|
| Team and class participation | 15 points |
| Activity 1: Story Specs | 40 points |
| First page of script | 20 points |
| Activity 2: The Pitch | 20 points |
| Self-Assessment and Reflection | 5 points |

## Extension Activities

- Explore the art of persuasion in more detail starting with Aristotelian appeals to logos, pathos, and ethos.
- Look at persuasive speeches or "pitches" in literature. (Example: Marc Antony's speech that begins "Friends, Romans, countrymen, lend me your ears" from Shakespeare's *Julius Caesar*)

## NCTE/IRA Standards Connection

4. Students adjust their use of spoken, written, and visual language (e.g., conventions, style, vocabulary) to communicate effectively with a variety of audiences and for different purposes.

5. Students employ a wide range of strategies as they write and use different writing process elements appropriately to communicate with different audiences for a variety of purposes.

6. Students apply knowledge of language structure, language conventions (e.g., spelling and punctuation), media techniques, figurative language, and genre to create, critique, and discuss print and non-print texts.

# The Perfect Pitch

## Answer Key
### Check Yourself! Skill Check

1. A logline is one or two sentences that describe the basic premise of a show or movie idea. Examples will vary.

2. Answers will vary. Sample answers: saying too little or too much; writing a poor letter; not grabbing the reader or listener in the first few sentences; describing a movie as "this movie meets that movie;" making a wild claim about how successful the movie will be; appealing to pity or referencing past rejections.

3. Answers will vary. Sample answers:

   a. It was obvious the dog had eaten the bone./The dog had obviously eaten the bone.

   b. "more superior"

   c. "slow as molasses"

   d. "held back" (failed), "bit the dust" (died)

4. Our hero finds himself at the bottom of a ravine, in dire straits, where he wanders lost for four days.

# The Perfect Pitch
## Expedition Overview

### Challenge
You have toiled over your movie screenplay for two years. You know it's box office gold, but how do you get people to look at it? You need the perfect pitch! For this project, you will develop a movie idea and create the written materials that will sell it for you.

### Objectives
- To practice writing concise, yet powerful, descriptive sentences
- To effectively outline important elements of a story or story idea
- To learn how to write a professional and persuasive query letter

### Project Activities
**Before You Go**
- Making Every Word Count

**Off You Go**
- Activity 1: Story Specs
- Activity 2: The Pitch

### Expedition Tools
Story Specs sheet

### Other Materials Needed
computer with Internet access

### Lingo to Learn—Terms to Know
- antagonist
- logline
- pitch
- protagonist
- synopsis

# The Perfect Pitch

## Expedition Overview

### Helpful Web Resources

- Crafty Screenwriting: Writing Movies That Get Made—Query Letters
  www.craftyscreenwriting.com/query.html

- Guide to Grammar and Writing: Writing Concise Sentences
  http://grammar.ccc.commnet.edu/grammar/concise.htm

- The Internet Movie Database
  www.imdb.com

- Project Greenlight
  http://projectgreenlight.liveplanet.com

- Screenwriter's Utopia
  www.screenwritersutopia.com
  Includes author/screenwriter interviews and screenwriting contests.

- Two Adverbs
  www.twoadverbs.com

# The Perfect Pitch

## Before You Go

## Making Every Word Count

| | |
|---|---|
| **Goal:** | To learn how to convey ideas powerfully using a limited number of words |
| **Materials:** | computer with Internet access |

A logline is a one- or two-sentence description of a movie. It may be the only sentence that an agent, an executive film developer, or a producer ever has time to read or hear. A good logline often describes the movie on two levels:

- the who, what, and how of what literally happens
- the deeper significance, theme, or story

Example: A young girl is invited to dine with a wolf disguised as a kind old woman and learns too late never to talk to strangers.

## Directions

1. Many people think writing a lot is difficult. In fact, writing *a little* may be the more difficult challenge. Loglines and movie pitches are great examples. You can't say too little, and you can't say too much. Brainstorm a list of movies you have seen recently and write a logline for each one.

   a. Movie name:_____

   Logline: _____

   _____

   b. Movie name:_____

   Logline: _____

   _____

   c. Movie name:_____

   Logline: _____

   _____

# The Perfect Pitch

## Before You Go

d. Movie name:_____

   Logline: _____

   _____

e. Movie name:_____

   Logline: _____

   _____

f. Movie name:_____

   Logline: _____

   _____

2. Exchange loglines with another student. Discuss. Are the loglines concise? Are they powerful enough to hook someone's interest? What edits might improve them? Provide feedback.

3. Review tips for writing concise sentences on the Guide to Grammar and Writing web site (http://grammar.ccc.commnet.edu/grammar/concise.htm). Be sure to take the three practice quizzes on the site.

# The Perfect Pitch
## Off You Go

## Activity 1: Story Specs

| | |
|---|---|
| **Goal:** | To elaborate on the basic plot, central conflict, or main character of a movie |
| **Tools:** | Story Specs worksheet |
| **Materials:** | computer |

Develop an idea for a movie! Choose a theme, a scenario, a dramatic conflict, or a character profile from literature you have read this year and develop a new story based on it. Alternatively, work on an original idea from your own imagination. Record information on your Story Specs worksheet or attach it.

### Story Spec Guidelines

You do not need to write the complete screenplay. Create the following materials only:

❏ an overview of the basic idea

❏ a description of the central conflict, obstacle, or problem

❏ a detailed sketch/profile of one character (protagonist or antagonist)

❏ the first page of your script

## Directions

1. Brainstorm ideas. Review interesting characters, plots, and issues from novels you have read recently. Browse the screenwriting competition sites listed under Helpful Web Resources to see examples of winning scripts.

2. Work through the story. What happens in the beginning, middle, and end? When and how do we meet the main character(s)? Is there a twist or a surprise at the end? Imagine key scenes unfolding. What is the turning point or climax? Make a graphic organizer (an outline, a cause-effect chart, a story development map, a character development map) or keep notes.

# The Perfect Pitch

## Off You Go

3. Write an overview of the idea and a description of the central problem. Be straightforward, clear, and concise.

4. Write the character profile. This requires more work. You have a limited amount of space (six to eight sentences) to deliver a gripping characterization. Who is the character? What is he or she like and why? What is the character's back story? What about him or her would most interest or intrigue an audience?

5. Prepare to write the first page of your script. First, determine your goal—do you want a "soft" opening for your film or an attention-grabber? Use your web resources to find screenplays or examples of winning first pages on screenwriting competition sites.

6. Type a draft of the first page. Include a title and your name. Use a screenplay format.

---

**Screenplay Format**

- **scene heading (slugline):** tells where and when the scene will take place; written in ALL CAPS

- **action/description:** sets the scene or describes the setting; written in present tense

- **character name:** inserted before a character begins to speak; indented 3.5 inches from left margin and written in ALL CAPS

- **parenthetical:** action or verbal direction for actor, to be used sparingly; short and written in parentheses

- **dialogue:** what a character says out loud or to himself or herself; indented 2.5 inches from left margin

---

# The Perfect Pitch

## Off You Go

**Example**

EXTERIOR (EXT)—FOOTBALL STADIUM—BLEACHERS—DAYBREAK

Empty stadium, sun rising, silent except for footsteps and breathing of sweating, exhausted SAM MILLER running to the top of the bleacher stairs.

SAM
(aloud, to no one in particular)
Only 10 more to go.

ALIEN #1
(watching from top step)
The earthling approaches.

An alien ship slowly rises above the top of the stadium and hovers.

# The Perfect Pitch
## Expedition Tool

### Story Specs

Use this tool to help you develop key components of your movie idea. Attach the first page of your script and query letter to this sheet.

Basic idea of the movie: _____

_____

_____

_____

Central conflict or problem: _____

_____

_____

_____

_____

_____

Main character profile: _____

_____

_____

_____

_____

_____

_____

Synopsis: _____

_____

_____

_____

_____

_____

Logline: _____

_____

_____

# The Perfect Pitch
## Off You Go

## Activity 2: The Pitch

| | |
|---|---|
| **Goal:** | To develop a polished pitch for your movie idea |
| **Tools:** | Story Spec worksheet |
| **Materials:** | computer |

Now that you have your movie idea, you will develop the tools you need to pitch it and test them out. Create the following materials:

- a well-written, compelling synopsis of the film
- your logline—a one- or two-sentence summary of the film
- a one-page query letter

Add the synopsis and logline to your Story Specs worksheet and attach the query letter. Once set, you will meet with producers (your class) to pitch your movie.

## Directions

1. Write your synopsis. Your synopsis should be polished since it is your written pitch. Tell the whole story of the movie in a style guaranteed to hook people. Think in terms of a commercial, a preview trailer, or the description moviegoers will read in the paper.

2. Write your logline. Review good logline strategies from Making Every Word Count.

3. Write a draft of your query letter. The goal of the letter is to attract interest in your screenplay. Use your web resources to find tips on writing query letters.

> Here is the typical format of a query letter:
>
> - **opening paragraph:** the reasons you are querying this person; a hook about why the script will be of interest to him or her
>
> - **pitch:** what the movie is about and why it is interesting
>
> - **credentials:** brief information on your qualifications
>
> - **close or "handshake":** an invitation to read the script and instructions on how to get a copy (via your agent or you, and contact information)

4. Get feedback on your letter, revise as needed, and type the final copy.

5. Pitch your movie! Follow your teacher's instructions and be ready for a few unexpected pitch situations.

# The Perfect Pitch

## Check Yourself!

### Skill Check

1. What is a logline? Write a strong example for a movie you have seen recently.

   _____

   _____

   _____

2. What are some common mistakes a person might make pitching a movie idea (in writing or in person)? List at least four mistakes.

   _____

   _____

   _____

   _____

3. Give an example of each item below. Use your web resources to help you.

   a. expletive construction: _____

   _____

   b. unnecessary use of an intensifier: _____

   _____

   c. cliché: _____

   _____

   d. euphemism: _____

   _____

4. Rewrite the sentence below to make it more concise and appealing to the reader.

   > It is then that our hero finds himself at the bottom of the ravine in
   > an extremely dire situation, wandering hopelessly lost for a period
   > of four days.

   _____

   _____

   _____

# The Perfect Pitch
## Check Yourself!

### Self-Assessment and Reflection
**Project Management**

#### Before You Go

- ❑ I know what loglines are and have practiced writing them.
- ❑ I reviewed tips for writing concisely. I can identify issues that lead to poor, wordy sentences.
- ❑ I'm honestly not sure I understand the writing skills I need for this project and have asked my teacher for additional help.

#### Off You Go

- ❑ I reviewed the project challenge and project materials carefully and thoroughly. I understand the products I will produce: a movie idea; a description of the main conflict; a character sketch; the first page of a script; and a well-written synopsis, logline, and query letter.
- ❑ The information on my Story Specs worksheet is well-written, concise, and compelling. It is legible and contains no errors in grammar, spelling, or punctuation.
- ❑ The first page of my script is deliberate. I put thought into my strategy for the opening scene. My final page is typed in script format.
- ❑ My movie synopsis is concise, yet descriptive and complete. It explains all key elements of the movie in a way that grabs attention.
- ❑ My logline is one or two sentences of carefully crafted verbal artistry.
- ❑ I reviewed tips for writing a good movie query letter. My letter follows the recommended format and is a perfect pitch.
- ❑ I checked all written work and corrected any errors in grammar, spelling, or punctuation.

#### Do You Know?

- ❑ I can define the Lingo to Learn vocabulary terms for this project and give an example of each.
- ❑ I completed the Skill Check questions, and carefully reviewed questions I answered incorrectly.

# The Perfect Pitch

## Check Yourself!

**Reflection**

1. What were the most challenging aspects of this project for you and why?

   _____

   _____

   _____

   _____

   _____

   _____

   _____

2. What skills did this project help you develop?

   _____

   _____

   _____

   _____

   _____

   _____

   _____

3. If you did this project again, what might you do differently and why?

   _____

   _____

   _____

   _____

   _____

   _____

   _____

*Expeditions in Your Classroom: English Language Arts*

# Literary Ambassadors

## Overview
Students explore cultural and national identity as reflected in literature and in the perspective of overseas students.

## Time
Total time: 8 to 14 hours

- Before You Go—Understanding America: three to four 55-minute classes and one to two hours of homework

- Activity 1—What Do They Read In . . . ?: 60 to 90 minutes of homework and one 55-minute class

- Activity 2—Books Over Borders: three to five 55-minute classes and e-mail correspondence time

## Skill Focus
- themes in American and world literature
- cross-cultural communication

## Prior Knowledge
- analyzing point of view
- responding to literature

## Team Formation
Students can work individually or in teams of two to four students. This can also be a whole-class activity. Team formation will vary depending on how you choose to organize communication with students overseas.

## Lingo to Learn—Terms to Know
- **archetype:** an ideal example or model of a type after which other things are patterned; an example of a personality type
- **genre:** literary type or form
- **motif:** recurring subject, theme, or idea; dominant idea
- **stereotype:** a generalization used to describe a person or group, often exaggerated or oversimplified; suggestion or assumption that a person or thing is the same as all others of its type
- **symbol/symbolism:** literary device in which an object represents an idea

# Literary Ambassadors

## Suggested Steps
### Preparation

Determine how to identify and manage communication with overseas students. Suggestions:

- Establish connections with one or more overseas teachers through your own network. Communication can be done via e-mail or posted to a common web site. (For example, use a free online group list or blog service—Google Groups, Yahoo! Groups, Blogger, and so forth.) Individuals or student teams can use ePALS, Friendship through Education, or a similar online tool. The program helps you find students and manage communication. In this case, you may want to specify a country or region related to literature you are studying.

- Find two or three excerpts from American literature that you can use as examples for Before You Go: Understanding America (classic motifs, American archetypes, important American voices, and so forth). You may also want to find a passage from a non-American work to use as contrast.

- If the class will focus on one country and overseas class, find author examples in advance.

- Consider a fixed time line—for instance, students will correspond once a week for six weeks. Alternatively, you might let students correspond as often as they like for a semester or year.

### Day 1

1. Provide an overview of the project and review project materials.

2. Facilitate Before You Go: Understanding America. Start with a class discussion.

   - Ask students if they can identify important themes or characters (archetypes) from American literature. Discuss examples and whether or not they "say" something about America and Americans.
   - Prompt thinking by saying "If someone from China read this novel, what images or views about Americans might they be left with?"
   - Brainstorm a list of writers or works that seem to say something about America and American identity, past or evolving.

3. Review the instructions for Before You Go: Understanding America and assign a due date.

# Literary Ambassadors

**Homework**

Have students begin a search for examples of American writing.

**Days 2 and 3**

1. Have students continue their search for examples of American writing and review students' examples.

2. Highlight good examples. Discuss how students found samples and why they selected them. Look for common themes.

3. Have students begin work on their analysis essays.

**Homework**

Have students complete their analysis essays.

**Day 4**

1. Lead a classroom discussion based on passages students found. Have students read sections.

2. Ask students to think about what the pieces say about America or American identity. Identify common motifs, characterizations, and so forth.

3. Work with students to choose a subset of materials they would like to use for the next part of their project (sending examples to students overseas).

**Day 5**

1. Explain how students will connect with overseas students. Form teams and provide instructions (for example, how to find pen pals or create an online group site).

2. Introduce Activity 1: What Do They Read In . . . ?

3. If the class will focus on one country and overseas class, assign preselected authors to various teams. *Note:* You may also want to explain that popular authors might not be native-born (for instance, French authors for northern and western Africa). If you prefer, you can exclude these authors; however, leaving it open allows students to explore literary heritage more broadly.

# Literary Ambassadors

**Homework**

Have students complete country research.

**Day 6 through Correspondence Completion**

1. Discuss country research. Ask students to share interesting facts. Discuss initial perspectives on countries and cultures.

2. Explain Activity 2: Books Over Borders. Set a time line for communication (fixed, open until a finish date, etc.).

3. Emphasize that students are welcome to get to know their counterparts and socialize appropriately. However, remind students that they must cover the basic goals of the project (exchange literature and perspectives).

4. Review introductory questions prepared by students.

5. Launch communication! Check in periodically and discuss findings using Activity 2: Books Over Borders.

**Final Day**

1. Make sure there is an official finish to correspondence as it relates to the project. Have students thank their counterparts. If students wish to continue correspondence, ask them to let you know formally.

2. Assign the Skill Check questions. Review answers.

3. Direct students to complete the Check Yourself! Self-Assessment and Reflection worksheet and submit it (optional).

## Project Management Tips and Notes

- There are a number of ways you (or your students) can find an overseas school to work with (see Suggested Steps). A class in an international school is a good partner for those new to overseas collaboration.
- If students create their own connections, discuss appropriate parameters (for instance, overseas students must be part of a formal class, the teacher must be on board, etc.). Ask students to give you contact information for the student(s) and teacher.
- You may want to provide parents with information about the project and require permission slips.

# Literary Ambassadors

- Students overseas often have an amazing command of literature, but English-speaking skills will vary. You might have students review and revise initial messages to make sure they are clear and straightforward (students should avoid slang and so forth).
- Have an official start and finish correspondence. Students on both sides should be clear on the time line.

## Suggested Assessment

Use the English Language Arts Project Assessment Rubric or the following point system:

| | |
|---|---|
| Team and class participation | 15 points |
| Before You Go: Understanding America | 30 points |
| Activity 1: What Do They Read In . . .? | 20 points |
| Activity 2: Books Over Borders | 30 points |
| Self-Assessment and Reflection | 5 points |

## Extension Activities

- Try additional lessons on cross-cultural communication. Try the Peace Corps Culture Matters Workbook (www.peacecorps.gov/wws/educators/enrichment/culturematters/index.html).
- Have students read a complete novel from the country they're studying and ask their international counterparts about it.
- If this project is carried out as a whole-class activity, choose two works that the American class and the counterpart class can all read and discuss. In other words, choose one American author and one counterpart author (in translation).
- Conduct a video conference where students discuss their cultures as portrayed in literature and elsewhere.

## NCTE/IRA Standards Connection

1. Students read a wide range of print and non-print texts to build an understanding of texts, of themselves, and of the cultures of the United States and the world; to acquire new information; to respond to the needs and demands of society and the workplace; and for personal fulfillment. Among these texts are fiction and nonfiction, classic and contemporary works.

4. Students adjust their use of spoken, written, and visual language (e.g., conventions, style, vocabulary) to communicate effectively with a variety of audiences and for different purposes.

7. Students conduct research on issues and interests by generating ideas and questions, and by posing problems. They gather, evaluate, and synthesize data from a variety of sources (e.g., print and non-print texts, artifacts, people) to communicate their discoveries in ways that suit their purpose and audience.

9. Students develop an understanding of and respect for diversity in language use, patterns, and dialects across cultures, ethnic groups, geographic regions, and social roles.

11. Students participate as knowledgeable, reflective, creative, and critical members of a variety of literacy communities.

## Other Helpful Resources

- British Council enCompassCulture: How To Find a Reading Group Twin
  www.encompassculture.com/readinggroups/readinggrouptwin

- The Peace Corps Cross-Cultural Workbook: Culture Matters
  www.peacecorps.gov/wws/educators/enrichment/culturematters/index.html

## Answer Key
### Check Yourself! Skill Check

1. An archetype is an ideal example or model of a type after which other things are patterned, or an example of a personality type. (Examples: Robin Hood, Peter Pan) A stereotype is a generalization used to describe a person or group, often exaggerated or oversimplified, or a suggestion or assumption that a person or thing is the same as all others of its type. (Examples: "tall people are clumsy," the angst-ridden teen, the wise old man)

2. Imagery is descriptive language that creates an image in your mind (appeals to the senses); imagery is created using figures of speech such as similes, metaphors, and personification. Symbolism is the use of iconic representations or objects to suggest abstract concepts. They both relate to physical things—things often particular to a culture, such as foods, animals, and religious and historical artifacts. Alternatively, cultures ascribe different meanings to the same objects and symbols. (For instance, a "thumbs-up" symbol is a good thing in the United States but can be an insult elsewhere.)

3. Common motifs: the American dream realized or not; coming of age; innocence of youth; race/racism; the underdog. Archetypes: the trickster (Huck Finn, Bart Simpson); Willie Loman in *Death of a Salesman*; Ahab hunting the white whale in *Moby Dick*; the boss; the feminist; the aging rock star. Why they recur: They reflect nostalgia or an ongoing struggle; they are part of the nation's history and identity; they help convey shared meaning quickly.

# Literary Ambassadors
## Expedition Overview

## Challenge
Around the world, students like you are in classrooms reading and analyzing literature. But what do they read in China or in Egypt? In this project, you will communicate with students in another country to find out. You will explore the theme of cultural identity and the role literature plays in examining and nurturing that identity.

## Objectives
- To explore classic themes in American literature
- To learn about the literature and literary characters of another country and culture
- To explore perspectives another culture has on America, Americans, and American identity

## Project Activities
**Before You Go**
- Understanding America

**Off You Go**
- Activity 1: What Do They Read In . . . ?
- Activity 2: Books Over Borders

## Expedition Tools
Books Over Borders worksheet

## Other Materials Needed
computer with Internet access

## Lingo to Learn—Terms to Know
- archetype
- genre
- motif
- stereotype
- symbol/symbolism

## Helpful Web Resources
- British Council enCompassCulture: The Global Bookclub
  www.encompassculture.com

- The E Pluribus Unum Project: Who is this American?
  www.assumption.edu/ahc/Intros/introamericanid.html

# Literary Ambassadors
## Expedition Overview

- ePALS Book Club
  www.epals.com/projects/book_club

- ePALS Instant Translation tool
  www.epals.com/translation/translation.e

- Friendship Through Education
  http://friendshipthrougheducation.org

- Frommer's Travel Guides
  www.frommers.com

- The Library of Congress: Country Studies
  http://lcweb2.loc.gov/frd/cs/cshome.html

- The Nobel Prize in Literature
  http://nobelprize.org/nobel_prizes/literature

- Peace Corps: Worldwise Schools
  www.peacecorps.gov/wws

- U.S. Department of State: Key Sites on American Literature
  http://usinfo.state.gov/products/pubs/oal/amlitweb.htm

- U.S. Department of State: Office of Overseas Schools—Schools by Regions
  www.state.gov/m/a/os/c1684.htm

- U.S. Department of State: Writers on America
  http://usinfo.state.gov/products/pubs/writers

- University of California, Santa Barbara: Voice of the Shuttle
  http://vos.ucsb.edu

- Words Without Borders: The Online Magazine for International Literature
  www.wordswithoutborders.org

# Literary Ambassadors
## Before You Go

## Understanding America

| | |
|---|---|
| **Goal:** | To explore works that reflect American literary tradition and perspectives |
| **Materials:** | computer with Internet access |

What do books, poems, and stories written by U.S. authors have to say about America and Americans—directly or indirectly? Which authors have written something that perfectly captures American culture?

## Directions

1. Choose a passage from a novel, a poem, an essay, song lyrics, or a scene from a play by an American author. The piece of writing must do one or more of the following:

   - describe an important aspect of America or of American culture
   - reflect an important American value or viewpoint
   - represent an essential voice
   - provide an example of "classic" or contemporary American writing

2. Analyze your selection and write a short review of it (four or five paragraphs). Aside from the obvious (it was written by an American), what makes this piece so "American"? What does it say about the country and the American people? Your essay should be typed and should include the following:

   - author
   - title
   - short summary or overview of the piece—what it is about, who it is about, and where it fits into the overall story or novel
   - your analysis

3. As a class, discuss selections. Use the following questions to guide your discussion:

   - What do the pieces/writers say about American identity?
   - Are there any common motifs, symbols, or archetypes?
   - What shapes American identity? Have authors helped do this?
   - Why would it be important for someone who is not from the United States to read these pieces?

4. Choose six to eight of the most interesting or representative choices. You will share these with students in another country later.

# Literary Ambassadors

## Off You Go

## Activity 1: What Do They Read in . . . ?

| | |
|---|---|
| **Goal:** | To learn about the country, culture, and literary heritage of exchange partners |
| **Materials:** | computer with Internet access |

## Directions

1. Find out where your international counterparts are from (country and city) and find the location on a map.

2. Use your web resources to read about the country and its culture. If possible, take a virtual tour. Record your notes below.

   Interesting facts about the country and culture:

   _____

   _____

   _____

   _____

   _____

3. Research one author from the country. Record your notes below.

   International Author Profile

   Author name: _____

   Country: _____

   Date of birth/death: _____

   Biographical information:

   _____

   _____

   _____

   _____

   _____

*Expeditions in Your Classroom: English Language Arts*

# Literary Ambassadors
## Off You Go

Literary contribution (What is the author known for?):

_____

_____

_____

_____

_____

Best-known works:

_____

_____

_____

# Literary Ambassadors
## Off You Go

## Activity 2: Books Over Borders

| | |
|---|---|
| **Goal:** | To exchange cultural and literary information with students from another country |
| **Tools:** | Books Over Borders worksheet |
| **Materials:** | computer with Internet access |

## Directions

1. Prepare to meet your international counterparts! Write three to five paragraphs you can use to introduce yourself and your community. You might also want to make a short list of introductory questions you want to ask your partner.

2. Make contact. Follow your teacher's instructions on how to connect and communicate with your partner.

3. Explain that you are interested in learning about your partner's culture, through his or her eyes and those of writers from his or her country. Explain that you are curious about your partner's view of America and would like to send samples of writing you think really capture America and Americanism. Ask your partner to send examples from his or her culture that you can read and discuss.

4. Review the collection of passages you collected as a class in Before You Go: Understanding America. Choose examples to send.

   If your partner is a strong English speaker, you might send a large assortment, including many long passages. Students in the other country could read them all or divide them up. If your counterpart has limited English ability, consider sending fewer examples and shorter passages. Consider poems.

   Each time you send a passage, explain what it is and why you thought it was an interesting choice of American literature to send. Include a few questions you hope to discuss after your partner reads it.

5. Encourage your partner to send examples of passages written by well-known authors in his or her culture. Ask your partner to list favorite authors and books. Go to the library to find and read examples from the suggested list.

# Literary Ambassadors
## Off You Go

6. Pose questions to your counterpart about the literature he or she reads. The following are examples:

   - What do you read in school?
   - What do you read for fun?
   - How important are books or stories in your culture?
   - Is there a form or style of literature that is very important to your culture (ghazal, haiku, existential writing, didactic poetry, etc.)?
   - What are topics, themes, motifs, or values authors write about and why? What are some common symbols or references?
   - Who are well-known or beloved characters? Are there any archetypes?
   - What books are popular now? If your country has a best-seller list, what are examples of books on the list?

7. International Book Group (optional): Ask your partner to recommend one book for you to read—something published or translated into English that he or she has read or is reading. Read the book and discuss it.

8. Keep notes about what you learn using your Expedition Tool: Books Over Borders.

# Literary Ambassadors

## Expedition Tool

### Books Over Borders

What students from my partner's country read for school:

_____
_____
_____
_____
_____

What students from my partner's country read for fun:

_____
_____
_____
_____
_____

Important authors in my partner's country:

_____
_____
_____
_____
_____

Favorite literary characters or character types in my partner's country:

_____
_____
_____
_____
_____

*Expeditions in Your Classroom: English Language Arts*                    ©2007 Walch Publishing

# Literary Ambassadors
## Expedition Tool

Aspects of the country's culture conveyed in literature (symbols, common references, values, etc.):

_____

_____

_____

_____

_____

My understanding of the country's culture before the project:

_____

_____

_____

_____

_____

My understanding of the country's culture during and after the project:

_____

_____

_____

_____

_____

Some things about my culture that my counterpart might have learned:

_____

_____

_____

_____

_____

# Literary Ambassadors

## Check Yourself!

### Skill Check

1. What is the difference between an archetype and a stereotype? Give an example of each.

_____

_____

_____

_____

_____

_____

_____

2. Imagery and symbolism can vary widely in literature from different cultures. What are these devices and why are they so rooted in culture and place?

_____

_____

_____

_____

_____

_____

_____

3. Give an example of a common motif in American literature. Why do you think it recurs?

_____

_____

_____

_____

_____

_____

_____

*Expeditions in Your Classroom: English Language Arts*                    ©2007 Walch Publishing

# Literary Ambassadors

## Check Yourself!

### Self-Assessment and Reflection
Project Management

### Before You Go

- ❏ I understand the concepts of *motif* and *archetype*.
- ❏ I can give examples of classic American literary themes and characters.
- ❏ I can discuss the concept of American identity in literature and how authors have reflected it and shaped it.
- ❏ I'm honestly not sure I understand how to analyze the theme of American identity in literature and have asked my teacher for help.

### Off You Go

- ❏ I reviewed the project challenge and project materials carefully and thoroughly. I understand the requirements of products I need to create: an analytical essay on a passage from American literature, country research, and a worksheet that describes what I learned during discussions with my international counterpart.
- ❏ My essay meets the required criteria. It is thoughtful, uses specific examples from the text to support points, and contains no errors in spelling, grammar, or punctuation.
- ❏ My country research provides interesting, readable information written in my own words.
- ❏ If requested, I clearly outlined my plan and time line for communicating with my international counterpart and followed that plan.
- ❏ I prepared questions in advance that I could use to help stimulate conversation with my counterpart.
- ❏ I summarized interesting aspects and findings from our discussions on my Expedition Tool: Books Over Borders.

### Do You Know?

- ❏ I can define the Lingo to Learn vocabulary terms for this project and give an example of each.
- ❏ I completed the Skill Check questions and carefully reviewed questions I answered incorrectly.

# Literary Ambassadors
## Check Yourself!

**Reflection**

1. What were the most challenging aspects of this project for you and why?

   _____

   _____

   _____

   _____

   _____

   _____

   _____

2. What skills did this project help you develop?

   _____

   _____

   _____

   _____

   _____

   _____

   _____

3. If you did this project again, what might you do differently and why?

   _____

   _____

   _____

   _____

   _____

   _____

   _____

# Point for Point

## Overview

Students experiment with rhetorical techniques and hold a series of debates on class-related topics or current events.

## Time

Total time: 12 to 20 hours (four debates over four months)

- Before You Go—Clever Words: 60 minutes of homework and one 55-minute class
- Before You Go—Argument Aerobics: one 55-minute class
- Activity—Creative Controversy: five 55-minute classes over a year, 1 to 2 hours of homework per discussion

## Skill Focus
- speaking skills
- analytical skills

## Prior Knowledge
Familiarity with persuasive speaking is helpful.

## Team Formation
This is a class project. Teams will vary by debate format.

## Lingo to Learn—Terms to Know
- **ad hominem:** appealing to feelings instead of intellect
- **fallacy:** faulty reasoning; an argument with at least one error that makes the conclusion or final statement incorrect
- **premise:** assertion that forms the basis for an approach, a position, or an argument
- **rhetoric:** persuasive language; technique and rules for using language effectively
- **rhetorical device:** use of language to create a literary effect; figure of speech

## Suggested Steps
### Preparation

- Determine how often you will hold "creative-controversy" sessions, or debates (for example, once per month).
- Set up a "That's Debatable" suggestion box and instruct students to submit potential debates at will or as they come up in class discussions.

# Point for Point

- Write rhetorical terms on slips of paper and put them in an envelope. See Before You Go: Clever Words for terms. Add additional terms if desired.

## Day 1

1. Provide an overview of the project.

2. Show students the topic suggestion box if you will use one.

3. Begin Before You Go: Clever Words. Students look up rhetorical terms, or you can cover some or all in class. Provide computer lab time or assign questions as homework.

## Homework

Have students work on Before You Go: Clever Words.

## Day 2

1. Review rhetorical terms. Discuss examples or give an example and ask students to think of a similar one.

2. Facilitate Before You Go: Argument Aerobics. Call on two students at a time or mix things up. (For instance, if the first debate is between two students, the next debate can be between two teams.) See Other Helpful Resources for debate format variations.

3. For each debate, ask the pair or team to draw their topic and rhetorical term from a hat or an envelope. Have students return rhetorical terms so other teams choose them again.

## Day 3

1. Brainstorm or list possible debate topics.

2. Have the class discuss and select final topics. In cases where there is no clear for/against argument, develop a formal "resolution" you can use to structure the debate.

3. Schedule debate days.

4. Review the Expedition Tools—the Creative Controversy Prep Sheet and the Creative Controversy Evaluation. Discuss the terms *supporting point* and *evidence.*

# Point for Point

### Debate Prep

1. Instruct students to submit the Creative Controversy Prep Sheet at least one week in advance of each debate.

2. Review prep sheets. Use the information to determine the best teams and format for the debate. For example, create teams of like-positioned students or deliberately assign students who gave weak "against" positions to the "against" team. You might also flag exceptionally good points so that you, as discussion moderator, can call on the student for that point.

3. Identify a good format for the debate. Vary this from debate to debate. For example:

   - head-to-head debate (teams square off)
   - round robin (two teams start and the winning team debates the next team)
   - public forum (select students serve as panelists and others comment and question, or the forum is open to questions or comments from anyone; the teacher or a student is the moderator)
   - role-play debate (students assume the role of a person or a character involved)

   See Other Helpful Resources for additional format ideas. Your topic will often lend itself to a particular format.

4. Return prep sheets and give students their team/position assignments and format information.

### Debate Day

1. Make copies of the Creative Controversy Prep Sheet (one per student for the day or one per debate if you are pairing smaller teams for multiple debates).

2. Review debate format and rules.

3. Oversee the debate.

4. Allow 10 to 15 minutes for evaluations and debate debrief (strengths and weaknesses).

### Final Day

1. Assign the Skill Check questions.

2. Check and review answers.

3. Have students complete the Check Yourself! Self-Assessment and Reflection worksheet and submit it (optional).

# Point for Point

## Project Management Tips and Notes

The word *debate* is used loosely to cover a range of discussion scenarios in which students must prepare in advance to discuss for/against or pro/con positions. This is a flexible project and can be used in several ways: as a stand-alone unit/clinic on persuasion or debate; in parallel with existing units since Creative Controversy topics are drawn from literature themes (emphasis on preparing for key discussions, mixing up classroom discussion dynamics); or as preparation for a research project (emphasis on good research, strong supporting points, and so forth).

## Suggested Assessment

Use the English Language Arts Project Assessment Rubric or the following point system:

| | |
|---|---|
| Team and class participation | 25 points |
| Before You Go: Clever Words | 10 points |
| Expedition Tool: Creative Controversy Prep Sheets | 10 points each ($\times$ 4) |
| Expedition Tool: Creative Controversy Evaluations | 5 points each ($\times$ 4) |
| Self-Assessment and Reflection | 5 points |

## Extension Activities

- Hold an ongoing web-based debate related to a major theme of the class.
- Post a current event or literature-based topic and ask students to weigh in regularly as their knowledge of the topic evolves.
- Discuss active-listening skills and how *not* to argue (common discussion and debate faux pas).

## NCTE/IRA Standards Connection

1. Students read a wide range of print and non-print texts to build an understanding of texts, of themselves, and of the cultures of the United States and the world; to acquire new information; to respond to the needs and demands of society and the workplace; and for personal fulfillment. Among these texts are fiction and nonfiction, classic and contemporary works.

4. Students adjust their use of spoken, written, and visual language (e.g., conventions, style, vocabulary) to communicate effectively with a variety of audiences and for different purposes.

# Point for Point

7.  Students conduct research on issues and interests by generating ideas and questions, and by posing problems. They gather, evaluate, and synthesize data from a variety of sources (e.g., print and non-print texts, artifacts, people) to communicate their discoveries in ways that suit their purpose and audience.

8.  Students use a variety of technological and information resources (e.g., libraries, databases, computer networks, video) to gather and synthesize information and to create and communicate knowledge.

## Other Helpful Resources

- Education World: Debates in the Classroom
  www.educationworld.com/a_curr/strategy/strategy012.shtml

- Education World: More Resources for Classroom Debates
  www.educationworld.com/a_lesson/lesson/lesson304b.shtml

## Answer Key
### Before You Go: Clever Words

1.  Rhetoric is the art of persuasion through the use of oral language, often in a public setting.

2.  Answers will vary. Sample answer:
    Logos (reason): You don't have a cart and you could use it to haul your goods to market.
    Pathos (emotion): This cart will save you hours of backbreaking toil and leave you more time to enjoy life.
    Ethos (speaker's character): I have used this cart, and it would be of huge benefit to you also.

3.  A logical fallacy is an argument flawed in logic that makes the whole argument invalid. Issues inclue faulty assumption or fact, issue with relevance, faulty reasoning, and ambiguity.

4.  introduction: narration—relevant background material
    confirmation: presentation in logical order of the claims that support thesis, from strongest to weakest
    refutation and concession: consideration of opposing viewpoints; anticipation of objections without weakening the thesis
    summation: strong conclusion emphasizing the power and value of the argument

5. Dialectic is the exchange of propositions (theses) and counter propositions (antitheses) resulting in a synthesis; the resolution of a disagreement or the creation of new knowledge through rational discussion. Examples will vary.

6. Answers will vary. Possible answers: creating a dichotomy (black/white issue); reframing (only two sides); using a story or an anecdote; finding common ground with an opponent (Ransberger Pivot); using the rule of three (three points, three examples in a sentence); using syllogism.

**Expedition Tool: Rhetorical Terms**

Examples will vary.

1. appealing to feelings instead of intellect

2. a comparison that shows a similarity

3. opposite; emphasizes the contrast in ideas by using an obvious contrast in words within a parallel grammatical structure

4. the raising of an issue by seeming to pass over, ignore, or deny it

5. deliberate exaggeration (versus understatement)

6. the raising of a question the listener may have and then answering it

7. the deliberate use of understatement for emphasis or effect

8. a combination of contradictory words

9. a statement with two seemly contradictory parts that may nonetheless be true

10. similarity of structure in a pair or series of related words, phrases, or clauses

11. question that is asked for effect, not for the purpose of eliciting an answer but to assert or deny something obliquely

12. a type of logical argument that consists of a major premise, a minor premise, and a conclusion

13. figure of speech in which a part, member, or characteristic is used to mean the whole

14. the use of redundant language that adds no information; needless repetition of an idea

# Point for Point

**Check Yourself! Skill Check**

1. A syllogism is a type of logical argument that consists of a major premise, a minor premise, and a conclusion. Example: Apes eat bananas. All intelligent animals eat bananas. Apes are intelligent.

2. a. synecdoche

   b. litotes

   c. analogy

3. Answers will vary. Sample answer:
   Adams emphasizes the strength of the case by saying that his clients have been defended ably and completely. He uses understatement to emphasize the point again ("leaves me scarcely anything to say") and makes it clear that any "imperfection" in his argument couldn't dent the case. He then states the obvious ("this Court is a Court of JUSTICE") as if he can continue on the assumption that true justice will be served. He then deftly questions the assumption and suggests that the court review the concept of justice (and this is what he goes on to do, using a conception of justice that clearly underscores the rights and freedoms he is arguing for his clients).

# Point for Point
## Expedition Overview

## Challenge
Do you prefer to avoid conversational conflict, or do you love to take a position just for the sake of argument? Either way, this project will help you bulk up your rhetorical skills. You will explore tricks of the trade that go back thousands of years and test them out in a series of class debates.

## Objectives
- Use rhetorical techniques to structure an argument or emphasize a point.
- Learn how to research and represent a position.

## Project Activities

**Before You Go**
- Clever Words
- Argument Aerobics

**Off You Go**
- Activity: Creative Controversy

## Expedition Tools
- Rhetorical Terms
- Creative Controversy Prep Sheet
- Creative Controversy Evaluation

## Other Materials Needed
- computer with Internet access
- watch or timer

## Lingo To Learn—Terms To Know
- ad hominem
- fallacy
- premise
- rhetoric
- rhetorical device

## Helpful Web Resources
- About.com: Secondary School Educators—Active Listening
  http://712educators.about.com/cs/activelistening/a/activelistening_2.htm

- American Rhetoric: Rhetorical Figures in Sound
  www.americanrhetoric.com/rhetoricaldevicesinsound.htm

# Point for Point
## Before You Go

## Clever Words

| | |
|---|---|
| **Goal:** | To learn about persuasive technique and rhetorical devices |
| **Tools:** | Rhetorical Terms worksheet |
| **Materials:** | computer with Internet access |

## Directions
Use your web resources to learn about the history of logic and persuasion. Then answer the questions below.

1. What is rhetoric? _____

_____

_____

2. If Aristotle were trying to sell you a horse cart, what three types of appeals might he try? Give examples of what he might say.

_____

_____

_____

_____

_____

_____

3. What is a logical fallacy? What types of issues cause one?

_____

_____

_____

_____

_____

_____

# Point for Point
## Before You Go

4. What is the structure of the classical argument?

_____

_____

_____

_____

_____

5. What does the term *dialectic* mean? Give an example.

_____

_____

_____

_____

_____

6. What are other verbal tactics that can be used to make a point or to persuade?

_____

_____

_____

_____

_____

# Point for Point
## Expedition Tool

### Rhetorical Terms

Using your web resources to help you, define the following terms. Then give an example of each. If possible, give "live" examples drawn from what you actually see, hear, and read (conversations, talk-show programs, magazines, newspapers, etc.).

1. ad hominem: _____
   example: _____
   _____

2. analogy: _____
   example: _____
   _____

3. antithesis: _____
   example:_____
   _____

4. apophasis:_____
   example: _____
   _____

5. hyperbole:_____
   example: _____
   _____

6. hypophora: _____
   example: _____
   _____

7. litotes:_____
   example: _____
   _____

# Point for Point
## Expedition Tool

8. oxymoron: _____

    example: _____

    _____

9. paradox: _____

    example: _____

    _____

10. parallelism: _____

    example: _____

    _____

11. rhetorical question: _____

    example: _____

    _____

12. syllogism: _____

    example: _____

    _____

13. synecdoche: _____

    example: _____

    _____

14. tautology: _____

    example: _____

    _____

*Expeditions in Your Classroom: English Language Arts*

# Point for Point

## Before You Go

## Argument Aerobics

| | |
|---|---|
| **Goal:** | To practice using rhetorical techniques in actual discussions |
| **Materials:** | paper |

## Directions

1. Write down a silly but debatable topic on a slip of paper. Your teacher will collect it and add it to an envelope or a cup. Topic examples: liquid soap versus bar soap, smooth versus crunchy peanut butter, getting up early versus going to bed late

2. Your teacher will call on volunteers to step forward, choose a topic, and debate it.

3. You will also draw a second slip of paper—a rhetorical term that you must somehow incorporate into your technique. Class members will try to identify what you did and whether or not it helped you.

# Point for Point
## Off You Go

## Activity: Creative Controversy

| | |
|---|---|
| **Goal:** | To experiment with different styles of dialogue, debate, and rhetorical method |
| **Tools:** | Creative Controversy Prep Sheet, Creative Controversy Evaluation |
| **Materials:** | watch or timer |

You will experiment with different forms of debate and dialogue to develop your persuasive style and repertoire of rhetorical techniques. Use the following steps and the Creative Controversy Prep Sheet to prepare for the arguments to come.

## Directions

1. Make suggestions for debate topics. They may relate to literature you are reading, current events, life's big questions, or other subjects guaranteed to ignite discussion.

2. As a class, narrow suggestions down to four or five final topics, develop a resolution if necessary, and schedule debate dates (for example, one debate a month).

3. A week before the debate, submit a Creative Controversy Prep Sheet to your teacher.

> **Prep Sheet Guidelines**
>
> ❑ You must have a minimum of four strong supporting points, two for and two against (pros and cons). You will need to research both positions and may be asked to argue points contrary to your own beliefs.
>
> ❑ Include specific evidence to support each point and the *type* of evidence it is (for example, common sense, expert opinion, or research data).
>
> ❑ Include your view of fundamental issues accentuating the difference in viewpoints.
>
> ❑ You should have one or two rhetorical methods or tricks you want to experiment with during the discussion.

4. Your teacher will provide additional instructions and assignments for each debate session. You may need to do additional research to prepare.

5. Debate Days: Come prepared. If you need note cards, bring them. You will also be asked to use the Creative Controversy Evaluation to analyze the discussion.

# Point for Point
## Expedition Tool

## Creative Controversy Prep Sheet

Topic/Resolution:

| Two or more points **for** | | |
|---|---|---|
| Positions | Evidence | Evidence type |
| | | |
| | | |
| | | |
| | | |
| | | |
| **Two or more points against** | | |
| Positions | Evidence | Evidence type |
| | | |
| | | |
| | | |
| | | |
| | | |

Are any of these issues fundamentally behind the difference in views?

- understanding or interpretation of facts or data
- personal interests or needs
- differing values or belief systems

What one or two rhetorical techniques will you experiment with during this discussion?

_____

_____

_____

_____

_____

# Point for Point
## Expedition Tool

### Creative Controversy Evaluation

Use this tool to evaluate today's discussion and your contribution to it.

Today's topic: _____

Strongest points made: _____

_____

_____

_____

_____

Weakest points made: _____

_____

_____

_____

_____

Your contribution:

|  | Poor | Okay | Good | Excellent |
|---|---|---|---|---|
| **Clarity of points** | 1 | 2 | 3 | 4 |

- organized
- used evidence
- good rebuttal

|  | | | | |
|---|---|---|---|---|
| **Interaction** | 1 | 2 | 3 | 4 |

- considerate
- held own
- did not hog floor

|  | | | | |
|---|---|---|---|---|
| **Rhetorical technique** | 1 | 2 | 3 | 4 |

- good speaking style
- chose words for deliberate effect

# Point for Point
## Expedition Tool

Is there anything you need to work on for next time?

_____

_____

_____

_____

_____

_____

Overall, how did today's discussion go? What worked and what didn't?

_____

_____

_____

_____

_____

_____

# Point for Point
## Check Yourself!

### Skill Check

1. What is a syllogism? Give an example. _____

   _____

   _____

   _____

   _____

2. What rhetorical device does each of the following use?

   a. The United States will not attend the international summit. _____

   b. This little old quiz won't count for much. _____

   c. Hope springs eternal. _____

3. In 1841, John Quincy Adams served as defense attorney for the famous Amistad case heard by the Supreme Court. Here is an excerpt from his opening statement:

   I therefore proceed immediately to say that, in a consideration of this case, I derive, in the distress I feel both for myself and my clients, consolation from two sources—first, that the rights of my clients to their lives and liberties have already been defended by my learned friend and colleague in so able and complete a manner as leaves me scarcely anything to say, and I feel that such full justice has been done to their interests, that any fault or imperfection of mine will merely be attributed to its true cause; and secondly, I derive consolation from the thought that this Court is a Court of JUSTICE. And in saying so very trivial a thing, I should not on any other occasion, perhaps, be warranted in asking the Court to consider what justice is.

   In your own words (with or without rhetorical device terminology), describe what rhetorical strategies and techniques Adams uses.

   _____

   _____

   _____

   _____

   _____

   _____

   _____

# Point for Point
## Check Yourself!

### Self-Assessment and Reflection
**Project Management**

### Before You Go

- ❏ I understand the term *rhetoric* and can give examples of common rhetorical devices.
- ❏ I am not sure I understand rhetorical devices and have asked my teacher for additional help.

### Off You Go

- ❏ I reviewed our project challenge and project materials carefully and thoroughly. I understand the requirements and products I must create: rhetoric research, class debate topics, and prep and evaluation sheets for each debate.
- ❏ I provided complete answers and definitions on Before You Go: Clever Words.
- ❏ My Creative Controversy Prep Sheets are legible, understandable, and reflect good research and analysis of points for and against the issue.
- ❏ I was fully prepared for class debates and discussions, and participated actively.
- ❏ I identified and deliberately tested various rhetorical techniques during debates.
- ❏ I evaluated each debate, including my own contribution, and used what I learned to prepare for the next debate.

### Do You Know?

- ❏ I can define the Lingo to Learn vocabulary terms for this project and give an example of each.
- ❏ I completed the Skill Check questions and carefully reviewed questions I answered incorrectly.

# Point for Point
## Check Yourself!

Reflection

1. What were the most challenging aspects of this project for you and why?

   _____

   _____

   _____

   _____

   _____

   _____

   _____

2. What skills did this project help you develop?

   _____

   _____

   _____

   _____

   _____

   _____

   _____

3. If you did this project again, what might you do differently and why?

   _____

   _____

   _____

   _____

   _____

   _____

# English Language Arts Project Assessment Rubric

| | Percent of grade | 4 (Excellent) | 3 (Good) | 2 (Fair) | 1 (Poor) |
|---|---|---|---|---|---|
| **Knowledge and skills specific to project** | | Defines all key vocabulary, with examples. Actively uses terms, methods, and skills, and transfers them to other situations and contexts. | Defines majority of terms, with examples. Majority of skills or methods are applied correctly. Sometimes transfers them to other situations or contexts. | Definitions and explanations are confusing or incorrect. Some skills are used correctly. | No evidence of knowledge or skill development. Few correct methods, few correct answers. |
| **Research** | | Work shows high-quality research on topic or theme. Research is used consistently to support main claims or points. Sources are reputable and cited correctly. | Work reflects solid research. Research is used to support most main claims or points. Sources are reputable and cited correctly. | There is little evidence of research, or research is used inconsistently to support claims or points. Citations are incorrect or incomplete. Sources are questionable. | There is no evidence of research. No citations are provided. |
| **Grammar, spelling, and punctuation** | | Excellent use of mechanics. Sentences are varied and well-constructed. Student reviews work methodically for errors. | Uses mechanics consistently. There is some variety in sentence construction. Student reviewed work for errors. | Inconsistent control of mechanics. Student reviewed work for errors. | There are serious errors. There is little or no attempt to check work. |
| **Writing** | | Purpose or argument is focused, well-presented, and insightful. Includes excellent supporting details. Shows creativity; uses a distinctive voice. | Purpose is clear and presented in an organized, engaging way. Includes relevant supporting details. | Purpose or argument is vague. Organization is weak or inconsistent. | Topic is unclear. There are few supporting details and little evidence of organization. |
| **Critical reading/ responding to literature** | | Provides excellent summaries of main ideas and themes. Pays close attention to detail and context. Contributes insightful questions and makes valid inferences about the author's meaning, purpose, or point of view. | Summarizes ideas and themes adequately. Pays attention to details and context. Questions and inferences reflect a good understanding of the author's purpose or point of view. | Can summarize action or characters, but struggles to summarize ideas and themes. Identifies details and context, but has difficulty interpreting information or drawing conclusions. | Cannot summarize ideas or themes. There is little or no attention to detail or context. Contributes little or nothing to discussion. |

# English Language Arts Project Assessment Rubric

| | Percent of grade | 4 (Excellent) | 3 (Good) | 2 (Fair) | 1 (Poor) |
|---|---|---|---|---|---|
| **Final product** | | Meets all criteria. Organization and information exceed expectations. Reflects excellent understanding of project content. | Meets all criteria. Organization and information presented clearly. Reflects good understanding of project content. | Meets most criteria. Some elements or components are missing. | Did not contribute; did not submit or is missing major components. |
| **Presentation** | | Completed within specific time. Evidence of preparation is obvious. Emphasizes most important information. All team members are involved. | Almost completed within time. Some preparation evident. Covers majority of main points. Not all team members involved. | Almost completed within time. Little preparation evident. Misses a number of important points. Not all team members involved. | Did not participate, no preparation, way under or over time, or information is confusing and disjointed. |
| **Teamwork** | | Workload divided and shared equally by all members. | Most members, including student, contributed fair share. | Workloads varied considerably. Student did not contribute fair share. | Few members contributed. Student made little or no contribution. |
| **Class participation** | | Contributed substantially. | Contributed fair share. | Contributed some. | Contributed very little. |